Advance praise for
Michael Catt, Sherwood Baptist Church and

Prepare for Rain

Many books tell us the "what" and some even tell us the "why." Thank you, Michael Catt, for writing about the "how." I appreciate your knack of cutting to the chase and telling it like it is. This book inspires me to motivate people to be involved in something bigger by showing me the footsteps of the vision for a local church.

Charles Lowery
President, Lowery Institute for Excellence

Vision, courage, creativity, excellence and faith are rarely combined in great quantities in a church. At the Sherwood Baptist Church under the inspired and gifted leadership of Michael Catt, we have seen this unique combination of qualities develop an unheard of expression of church ministry—the production and introduction of an excellent motion picture which captured the heart of our nation. This significant production unashamedly challenged viewers to integrity, perseverance, character and ultimately to faith in the Lord Jesus Christ.

Jimmy Draper
President Emeritus, LifeWay Christian Resources

"I am still amazed at the movies *Flywheel* and *Facing the Giants*. They are like 'the little engine that could.' Michael Catt took the impossible and let it be HIM-possible. I remember him saying that in a meeting one time, and now that statement is being lived out in front of all of our eyes. I am so excited that these movies and their stories are being published for the masses. Hooray for the dreamers that do not listen to the voice that says, 'It can't be done.' Congrats Michael, Alex and Sherwood for stepping out and doing the HIM-possible!"

Mark Harris
Contemporary Christian Artist and Songwriter

When I heard Sherwood's mission statement to *reach the world from Albany, Georgia,* I thought, "How nice." And then I met Michael Catt and his team, and I was bowled over by their fearless determination to do just that. Dust the cobwebs off the idealism of your youth. They've proven it can be done.

Julie Fairchild
Lovell/Fairchild Communications

Can churches makes changes without destroying themselves? Yes! Can church leaders see and follow new visions without making divisions? Yes! Does God still do the impossible when we trust Him and seek only to glorify Him? Yes! The exciting story of one such church is in this book, and the best thing is that it's not an 'exclusive.' It can happen wherever God's people exalt Jesus Christ, work together, share the Word, prayer, and step out by faith to follow the vision God gives them. Is there a price to pay? Yes—but the blessings are worth it."

Warren Wiersbe

The Christian journey is never about standing pat, but about stepping out by faith to do the impossible in the power of the Holy Spirit. Churches don't produce movies—unless they are willing to step out on such faith. Michael Catt is just the kind of pastor and man of "faith steps" that God can use. With the faithful members of Sherwood Baptist Church, the powerful message of hope and faith has been broadcast around the world.

This book tells of that journey and the lessons all believers can learn about walking by faith.

Richard Powell
Pastor, McGregor Baptist Church
Ft. Myers, Florida

"I love people with a global vision. Monuments are not erected to pessimists. Michael Catt is a visionary. *Facing the Giants* is a success because a leader allowed those around him to be creative. Michael is a 'giver' not a 'taker.' The remarkable success of this movie is not a surprise to me. It is just Michael Catt being Michael Catt! The story of *Facing the Giants* will bless and thrill you. Sherwood Baptist Church in Albany is a special place. After you read the book, go visit the church. It is a church filled with GIANTS for God!"

Roger Breland
Executive Director and Dean, Center for Performing Arts,
University of Mobile
Founder of TRUTH

Prepare for
RAIN

The Story of a Church that
Believed God for the Impossible

Michael Catt

CLC
PUBLICATIONS
Fort Washington, PA 19034

· Prepare for Rain ·

Published by CLC ❖ Publications

U.S.A.
P.O. Box 1449, Fort Washington, PA 19034

GREAT BRITAIN
51 The Dean, Alresford, Hants. SO24 9BJ

AUSTRALIA
P.O. Box 2299, Strathpine, QLD 4500

NEW ZEALAND
10 MacArthur Street, Feilding

ISBN: 978-0-87508-977-5

Scripture quotations unless otherwise noted are from the
New American Standard Bible ®,
copyright © 1960, 1962, 1963, 1968, 1971, 1972, 1973, 1975,
1977, 1995 by The Lockman Foundation.
Used by permission.

Contents

• *Acknowledgments* • 7

• *Introduction:* • 11

1 • Plowing the Field • 15

2 • Back-Door Revival • 25

3 • Facing My Own Giant • 39

4 • An Environment of Prayer • 55

5 • A Visionary Team • 65

6 • Attitude Is Everything • 79

7 • Relationships Are Essential • 91

8 • Plow the Field God Gives You • 109

9 • Growing Pains and Moviemaking • 123

10 • Connect with the Right People • 135

11 • Send the Rain • 147

12 • That's a Wrap • 165

• *From Our Inbox . . .* • 173

• *Endnotes* • 181

TO

The Members of Sherwood Baptist Church

You have loved me, prayed for me, encouraged me
and endured with me.

You have embraced my vision and passion for revival
and encouraging preachers.

There are bigger churches in our world,

but none better.

Acknowledgments

A BOOK like this would not be possible without the investment of others. I'm thankful for our church staff. They are the finest team I've ever served with. There are no free agents or superstars in the bunch. We are all servants. In particular, Jim McBride is not only the Executive Pastor; he is also a friend who sticks closer than a brother. I could not do what I do without him.

Debbie Toole has been my Administrative Assistant for fifteen years. She keeps up with my schedule and does countless things that make my life easier. She wants things done right and works to make it so.

Stephanie Thompson is my Research and Development Assistant. Steph has put in countless hours to get the pieces of this book together. She makes me look like a writer. I have known her since she was in the third grade and have watched her grow into a godly young woman. She joined our staff after finishing seminary and has been a blessing to me.

Daniel Simmons serves as Pastor of Mt. Zion Baptist Church here in Albany and is also my "co-pastor." We do so much together as churches. His friendship, preaching and wisdom are examples and encouragements to me. God has allowed us to build many bridges in the divided city in which we live.

James Pitman and Dave Fessenden at CLC Publications (Christian Literature Crusade) believed in this project and put it on the front burner. They have given incredible support and encouragement. Having worked with them on my book, *Reflections on the Gospels*, I was eager to work with them again. They have a passion for ministry that is bigger than publishing. When I think about CLC, I think about what Christian publishing should be.

All of the churches who have called me to serve on staff or as a pastor have been a part of making me who I am today. Some of the experiences were painful, while others were seasons of blessings. All have been part of God's refining and defining process in my life.

Roger and Linda Breland have been friends, encouragers and intercessors for my wife and me for over thirty years. Their vision and example of faith and personal sacrifice helped me to realize that I should never settle for status quo.

For fifteen years I served as a youth pastor. I am particularly grateful for three pastors I had the privilege of serving with Dr. Charlie Draper taught me the importance of expository preaching. Dr. Fred Lowery taught me what it meant to lead men. Dr. Nelson Price helped me to see the big picture. I have a part of their DNA in my spiritual blood. Their gifts and abilities have helped to shape my view of ministry and the pastorate.

The four men who have mentored and marked me the most are James Miller, Vance Havner, Ron Dunn and Warren Wiersbe. James Miller was my youth minister growing up. He is still a dear friend. He believed in me when no one else did. As a teenager I surrendered to the lordship of Christ under the preaching of Vance Havner. I doubt if I've ever preached a sermon without quoting him. What a prophet! I first heard Ron when I was in seminary. He and I became friends around the time Vance Havner died. Ron taught me more than any seminary class I ever took. His sermons on Isaiah 45 and mountain-moving faith have influenced this book and my life. He preached sixteen consecutive Bible Conferences for me before he died. Preaching his funeral was the hardest day of my life. Warren Wiersbe has been a God-send and a powerful influence in my life. He has helped me stay balanced. I never talk to him without having a pen and paper close by. Little did I know when we met in 1994 that a handshake would develop into a friendship that would have such an impact on my life. All four men share a common denominator: their love for the Word and the church, their commitment to prayer and their hope for revival. These men are my ministry mavericks. They taught me to think outside the box without thinking outside the boundaries of Biblical truth.

I'm grateful for other men who have believed in me. They have encouraged me to pursue God. They have reminded me the only person I have to please is the Lord Jesus. Men like George Harris, John Bisagno, Jimmy Draper, Don Miller, Lehman Strauss, Charles Lowery, Bill Stafford, Ken Jenkins, Gary Miller, Tom Elliff and Jay Strack have impacted my life in ways they will never know this side of eternity. I am, of all men, blessed.

My wife Terri and my daughters Erin and Hayley offer constant support. Terri has moved across this country in support of my calling to ministry. She's the one who pushed me to write a book about the church. This might have never happened without her. She is God's gift to me; she's my best friend. Erin and Hayley are the joy of my life. No dad could be more proud of his daughters. I love seeing what God is doing through their lives. God has blessed me with three wonderful ladies in my life.

The Lord Jesus has been better to me than I deserve. I hope you see the grace of God in these pages. When life comes to an end, there's a dash—a line between our date of birth and our date of death. It's what happens in that dash that determines if we will hear "Well done." I pray my life sentence will be that I was committed to Jesus as Lord and to preaching the Word without apology. I pray that somehow our church can be a catalyst for revival in our land.

Michael Catt
Sherwood Baptist Church
Albany, Georgia, May 2007

Introduction

*I*N THE movie *Facing the Giants*, Grant Taylor, a discouraged football coach at Shiloh Christian Academy, gets an unexpected spiritual lesson from Mr. Bridges, a prayer warrior. When the coach tells Mr. Bridges "I just don't see God at work here," the prayer warrior responds with a story:

> "Grant, I heard a story about two farmers who desperately needed rain. Both of them prayed for rain, but only one of them went out and prepared his fields to receive it. Which one do you think trusted God to send the rain?"
>
> "Well, the one who prepared his fields for it."
>
> "Which one are you? God will send the rain when He is ready. You need to prepare your field to receive it."

How do you prepare for rain? How do you cultivate the soil of your life in preparation for God's outpouring? How do you break up the unproductive ground? How do you wait both expectantly and patiently for God to act?

I want God to send the rain. I want to see Him work in my life; I want to see revival in the church. I want to embrace all God has for me. When I read the stories of awakenings and revivals of the past, I long for that to happen in my church and my lifetime. I long for history to become present tense. I want to prepare for rain and watch God send it.

———— ⌇ ————

I want God to send the rain.
I want to see revival in the church.
I want to embrace all God
has for me.

But I must admit there have been times that I felt as dry and discouraged as Grant Taylor, and I didn't see God at work. He *was* working, though not in the way I expected. God was preparing my heart for growth and revival by turning the plow in my life and uprooting things I didn't want to deal with. Like the parable of the sower in Matthew 13, the problem was not the sower or the seed, but the soil. My soil needed to be tilled.

I serve as pastor of Sherwood Baptist Church in Albany, Georgia—a congregation that has received a great deal of attention recently. The establishment of Sherwood Pictures in 2000 brought a visibility to this fifty-two-year-old fellowship that we never imagined possible. Through our first two movies, *Flywheel* and *Facing the Giants*, we've expanded the impact and influence of this local assembly far beyond our "Jerusalem." We are literally hearing of changed lives around the world.

I've been asked hundreds of times, "How does a church make a movie?" That is a tough question to answer, but I think it misses the point. A more relevant question is "How can I overcome my personal obstacles to believe God for something bigger than myself?" Along with that is another question: "How do I believe God for revival and awakening that so energizes and empowers the church that we see Him do the impossible?"

To answer these questions, I need to share with you my story and the story of Sherwood Baptist Church, a congregation that has learned to trust God for great things and no longer be content with the status quo.

Alex Kendrick (Coach Grant Taylor) and Ray Wood (Mr. Bridges) in "Prepare for Rain" scene from the movie *Facing the Giants*

1

Plowing the Field

SHERWOOD is only my second senior pastorate. My first was in a town of about 17,000 in the Midwest, where I served for three years. The church was the largest in the community, and it was historically influential. After almost a decade of decline, we were seeing new birth, new members and new life. God was moving.

At the same time, I felt like I was fighting a battle for survival. Like many churches, the deacon board wanted to run the church and treat the pastor like a hireling. But after a few difficulties, we could see that God was turning the old ship around.

I had received repeated requests from Sherwood Baptist Church to consider becoming their pastor, but I declined. I felt like my ministry was just starting at this church in the Midwest, and I had no desire to move on. For one thing my children were very young, and I didn't want to uproot my family. Besides, I didn't want to be one of those preachers always looking for "the bigger and better" every few years.

In August of 1989 the late Manley Beasley came to our church as a guest preacher on Sunday and Monday. He was the greatest man of faith I'd ever met. I had read and preached about living by faith, but Manley was the walking personification of it. He had survived incurable diseases and an untold number of health issues. When Manley spoke, people listened.

That weekend I shared with Manley about the church and how at times it was like rolling a rock uphill.

"You'll know when I'm through tonight if your ministry here is over."

While we were making headway, it seemed that my authority was constantly being challenged, and I felt on guard. On Monday night, before he preached, Manley walked up to me and said, "You'll know when I'm through tonight if your ministry here is over." You can imagine that I put my spiritual antenna up during that message! (I told my wife to pay attention because we might be packing and leaving town under the cover of night.)

Turning to Isaiah 6, Manley preached a message entitled "Who Wants to See the Glory of God?" It was one of those God-moments when you could sense the Lord's presence throughout the room. Twenty years prior the church had seen a great revival and movement of God. Surely this message would stir the coals and rekindle the fire. Who doesn't want to see God's glory, especially if they've made the effort to come back to church on a Monday night?

When the invitation was given, I thought surely no one could stay in the pew. Terri and I immediately went to the altar and began to pray. I could sense others had moved forward, but I wasn't sure who or how many. The invitation didn't last long. A few minutes later Manley walked off the platform, placed his hand on my shoulder and said, "Now you know."

With a crowd of about 400 present, the only people at the altar were the church staff and a few members of the congregation. Deacons sat in their seats seemingly unmoved; Sunday school teachers looked like they were ready to leave. When I faced the congregation, I saw blank stares—they were lined up in the pews, stone-faced and seemingly indifferent. I knew it was over; God had released me from that ministry.

Less than a month later, the search committee from Sherwood called for a fourth time to see if I would reconsider. God immediately began to turn my heart toward Sherwood, and I've never looked back. I became their pastor in December 1989. Sherwood is not perfect, but it's the greatest church I've ever been a part of. I've been in a number of other churches of all shapes and sizes, in the inner city and the suburbs, but I've never seen people allow the Spirit to work like they do at Sherwood.

This journey of faith has not been easy, and it has not happened overnight. We are maturing as a congregation while staying young in our hearts. There have been problems, but there always are, anywhere you go. Transitions have sometimes felt like train wrecks, but God has been sovereign and faithful through it all, and I've learned to trust Him every step of the way.

Cold Feet

But to tell you the truth, I almost never made it to Sherwood. The weekend we were to be introduced to the congregation, I began having second thoughts. I even went so far as to tell the pastor search committee that I would preach on Sunday, but I wasn't sure I should come as pastor. I don't know why I got cold feet. Maybe it was because God was uncovering an issue He wanted me to deal with up front—one that was serious enough that it couldn't wait.

The first hint of trouble came when some of the leaders in the church were joking about the fussing and fighting in long deacons meetings. There's always a grain of truth behind that kind of humor, and I certainly wasn't interested in coming into a situation like the one I was coming out of. I knew one thing: God had called me to shepherd and lead—not referee!

In my first deacons meeting as pastor, the problem became clear to me. The entire meeting consisted of reviewing a document they called a "deacon's digest," which was a summary of church purchases, programs and committee reports. They were functioning like an executive board or finance committee, and they had operated this way for years. We spent several minutes discussing three bids on vacuum cleaners. As I looked around the room, I had a strange thought: *I bet none of these guys ever uses a vacuum cleaner. If I want to know which vacuum cleaner to buy, I'll ask their wives!*

I came to realize that the deacons were good and godly men, but they had become wrapped up in tradition rather than Scripture regarding the role of a deacon. They needed to be Biblical in their thinking. I heard them talk about how they would leave meetings with knots in their stomachs; there was no joy in serving. They had hearts for ministry, but no one had ever shown them a better way of doing it. They needed to be freed up to serve the way the Lord designed it in Acts 6.

So at one of the next meetings early in my first year, I announced a "silent coup" to the deacons. I said it was crazy for us to (1) vote on money already spent, (2) act as a second finance committee or (3) be

I announced a "silent coup" to the deacons . . . We were going to change the way we did ministry.

known for fussing and fighting. We were going to change the way we did ministry to focus on widows and keep unity in the church.

Thankfully, the deacons understood what I was trying to do and were willing to take a chance with their new pastor. They had great respect for pastoral authority and were willing (some reluctantly) to give this a try.

It was one of the defining moments for the church. We discovered that Acts 6 still works. We are living proof that a 21st-century church can function, grow and minister using a first-century model.

Organizational Changes

Once we had reformed the deacon ministry, we began to prune the organization. The church had over sixty committees, but lacked focused direction. We had people "serving" on committees who didn't even know it! It was a classic example of an organization beginning to fall apart through lack of leadership. (The church had been without a senior pastor for some time.) It's not an intentional thing, but the momentum of a church rises and falls on leadership—especially pastoral leadership. While a ministry may hold its own, it cannot grow without direction.

We began to eliminate committees that did not help us fulfill the purpose, vision and mission of the church. Over the course of three years, we cut the number of committees from sixty-two to two. If a committee had not met in the past year, it was gone.

Now we don't have committees; we have ministry teams. We have lay leaders who serve as the finance team and help us administrate the budget. The personnel team is an advocate for the staff. They work hand-in-hand with me and our executive pastor. When necessary we form a task force that meets for a specific purpose and is disbanded when the job is completed. This has allowed us to engage people who are purposeful and passionate in certain areas of giftedness. It also keeps the structure of the church streamlined and fluid, so that we can quickly respond to new situations and challenges.

Alan Redpath said, "There is no revival possible in any fellowship without a price being paid,"[1] and we lost some people when we made these changes. They wanted the church to operate like a secular corporation and wanted to be in control. But the church is not a place for fleshly power and human control; it is a vessel for the power and presence of the Holy Spirit.

"The Worship Wars"

Another mountain we faced was what has commonly been called "the worship wars" (though it seems to me that using "worship" and "wars" in the same sentence is a denial of what worship is all about!). I loved our worship at Sherwood, but we needed to make some changes in our style without compromising Biblical truth. We wanted to reach our community, and you can't reach a community that is predominantly African-American with Southern Gospel music.

If we were going to reach our "Jerusalem," we needed to move forward with our music and worship. God was calling us to be a multi-generational and multi-racial church. We had to adjust in order to do that effectively, and it was clear that we needed to do a more "blended" service. It wasn't a radical change. We didn't throw out the hymns; we just added choruses and encouraged more freedom in worship.

I also began to teach on the subject of worship. We started teaching the choir that worship isn't a performance for the crowd but a means to glorify God and exalt His name. I told the congregation that while we all have preferences in our music, we can be guilty of worshiping our preferences more than the Lord. Just because I like something doesn't mean it's God-honoring. True worship really has nothing to do with styles or preferences. A. W. Tozer wrote, "An active effort to close the gap between the heart and the God it adores is worship at its best."

This transition wasn't easy, but we did it without a split and without losing half the church. Some people didn't like the choruses, even though most of them were verses of Scripture put to song. Others didn't like the changes in worship initially, but they put "self" aside and trusted the leadership of the church. One of our members said, "It was hard to make that change. It's not that we didn't like it, we just weren't used to it."

We're still learning how to worship. We're still learning how to pray. We're still learning what it means to be a God-glorifying church. We haven't arrived, but we are further down the road than when we started. We have learned that worship is not about hymns versus choruses. It's not a matter of my way versus your way. It's not about gimmicks, manipulation or coercion. Worship is a matter of the heart.

Worship is not about hymns versus choruses. Worship is a matter of the heart.

Sherwood is not a perfect church. However, we've had preachers and visitors from all over the country, and they all say the same thing: "There's something special about this place. You can sense the Spirit of God here." Isn't that what we all want? Just like the rain, we need a refreshing downpour from heaven. We need to be washed of our doubt and fears. We need to be drenched in an abiding awareness of His grace, glory and power.

While we were in the midst of making these changes, Don Miller, a great prayer warrior, came to Sherwood for a four-day prayer conference. Every night of the conference the church was packed. One evening Don and his wife Libby came to our home after the service. We were sitting in my living room when Don asked, "Michael, are you ready to lose 800 people to see God really do a work in this church?"

Thinking that would never happen, I replied almost flippantly, "Yes. I'm willing to do whatever it takes to see God work in this church." I mean, come on, who ever heard of such a back-door route to revival? There was no way we were going to lose 800 people!

Little did I know . . .

Sherwood Baptist Church

2

Back-Door Revival

*L*ITTLE DID I know when I told Don Miller I was willing to lose 800 people to see revival that we would lose at least that many through several "back-door revivals" over the next ten years. Fortunately, we've never had a divisive business meeting, let alone a church split, but we have experienced some noticeable exoduses.

If you want to see how quickly God can crush your fleshly ego, tell Him you're willing to lose half of your congregation to see revival. He might test you on it. He certainly tested me. He pulled the rug out from under me. He broke me, dealt with my pride and reminded me of my spiritual heritage. I was taken back to commitments made years before.

When I was in high school, Vance Havner came to my home church. The great revivalist from the hills of North Carolina made a lasting impact on my life. On youth night (he was seventy-two at the time) he preached a message that marked me for life. He called on the young people to get the hymnal out and turn to "I Have Decided to Follow Jesus":

I have decided to follow Jesus.
I have decided to follow Jesus.
I have decided to follow Jesus.
No turning back. No turning back.

The world behind me; the cross before me.
The world behind me; the cross before me.
The world behind me; the cross before me.
No turning back. No turning back.

Havner then said, "If that's the desire of your heart and if you are willing to mean business for God, I want you to come to the altar and face this congregation and sing these words to them. I'm not interested in your voice; I want to hear your heart. I don't want any duets, quartets or ensembles. I want soloists. You'll come one at a time and make your confession of surrender."

I was the second one up, and I knew I would never be the same. I can't tell you how much that moment has meant to me in times when it would have been easier to compromise.

When people started to leave Sherwood because they disagreed with changes, I would remember that night from my youth. I also remembered times of fellowship with Havner as he mentored me, wrote to me and prayed for me. I had to follow Jesus no matter the cost.

By His grace, they did not all leave at once, but they did leave. Some left over a certain Bible translation. Some left when we moved toward a blended worship service with hymns and choruses. Some left to follow a staff member.

Some left because they didn't like strong preaching and didn't want to deal with their sin. Some left when I said that you aren't counted faithful by just coming to church one hour a week. Others left for unknown reasons, but they left.

And no matter the reason, the giant of pride, ego and comparison was always looming around the corner. Too often Christian leaders are guilty of the "look good at all costs" syndrome. We want to appear on top of our game at our denominational meetings. We want an impressive résumé for our next church. We are interested in numbers, nickels and noses.

After all, the first question you get when you are with your peers is, "How many are you running in Sunday school? How many are you baptizing?" We want others to

We may be bleeding on the inside, but we don't want our peers to know it.

think well of us. We may be bleeding on the inside, but we don't want our peers to know it. As a pastor it is hard to let your guard down. We've been taught, "Never let them see you sweat. Never admit you have a need. Be on top of your game."

However, if we are going to see revival and awakening in our lifetime, something has to change. The fact that repentance, holiness, sanctification and seeking the Lord are not popular is all the more reason for preaching it. We have got people seeking after feelings instead of the Father. Our pews are full of people with "Do Not Disturb" seemingly tattooed on their foreheads. The fact that today's "church-lite" mentality cannot endure sound doctrine is all the more reason to preach it. It is not the duty of a pastor to make the Word acceptable; it's his duty to make it available.

Vance Havner wrote,

> We have too many casual Christians who dabble in everything but are not committed to anything. They have a nodding acquaintance with a score of subjects but are sold on nothing. "Of course I'm interested in church—but with my club and my lodge and my golf and my bride and my stamp collecting and my ceramics and my African violets, I just can't get too excited about religion." Our Lord had no place in His program for casual disciples. It was all or nothing.[1]

Confronting Legalism and Gossip

During my first two years as pastor at Sherwood, we were growing at a rapid pace. It seemed we could do nothing wrong. Hundreds joined, and we were baptizing new believers almost every week. There was energy and excitement everywhere. It would have been easy for me to say, "Don't make any changes; just ride the wave."

But in my heart I wasn't comfortable. There was a pocket of legalism in the church, and I knew I had to confront it. I've come to believe it's easier for an alcoholic to be converted than it is to soften the heart of a hard-core legalist.

I was a product of the Jesus Movement of the late '60s and early '70s. The church by and large wasn't ready to embrace people who were converted during that time. I wanted to see a movement like that again. I had been influenced and impacted by the life and ministry of Vance Havner, A.W. Tozer, Leonard Ravenhill and others. I longed for a movement of God in every place God took me. I wanted to see the Spirit of God move among us in unexplainable ways.

Too many churches, however, don't want God to upset their system. They have their rules, programs and methods, and God forbid that a wind from somewhere else would blow in and disturb the status quo.

I unexpectedly rattled that status quo at Sherwood during one service in January of 1990. I hadn't asked anyone about Sherwood's view on clapping because I thought it was a minor point. To me it wasn't a matter of fellowship; it was a response of worship. After one particular choir special, I started clapping, not for the performer, but in praise to the Lord. There was a spattering of applause in the room, but I could immediately sense this hadn't been done before.

A man came to my office first thing Monday morning to confront me about it.

"Don't you know that clapping is a sin?" he asked.

When I quoted the Scripture that says, "Oh, clap your hands, all you peoples! Shout to God with the voice of triumph!" (Ps. 47:1), he said that was Old Testament and didn't apply to the church now. I then pointed out that the Old Testament is full of Christ, that Christ honored the Old Testament and that almost every book in the Old Testament is quoted in the New Testament. His response was shockingly eye opening.

"I didn't come here to argue the Bible with you, preacher. I know what I believe."

I was so struck by the legalism, self-righteousness and arrogance among a small group of people in the church that I knew I would have to address it.

It was not a new problem. The former pastor was criticized for living in a house in the neighborhood of the local country club, and Sherwood was quickly labeled a "country club" church! I was told when I moved here, "Don't buy a house in that neighborhood. People will talk."

The tongue-wagging continued well into my pastorate. One of the funny rumors that went around in my first year was that I had an airplane and was flying around the country. I don't even like to fly! In fact, I heard that one so much that I made a joke about it, telling the congregation we were expanding the parking lot so I could land my personal helicopter at the church. That backfired, of course, and I got reprimanded for wanting to cut down trees to expand the parking lot!

Why Mess with Success?

Soon it became apparent that the church was going to plateau if we didn't go deeper with the Lord. We looked spiritual on the surface, but underneath there were issues and sins that had never been addressed. As I preached through the Scriptures, these things began to surface, and it wasn't pretty.

By all outward appearances, we were successful. Why mess up a good thing?

One thing that came to light, for example, was that a handful of leaders in the church were not respected in the community because of their business practices. Their images were different than their substance.

I wrestled with what we should do—or if I should do anything at all. By all outward appearances, we were successful. We had been a leader among churches in our area in baptisms, new members and giving, year after year. Why mess up a good thing?

It was at a conference with Jim Cymbala and Warren Wiersbe that God spoke to my heart. I realized I had not let go of my agenda completely. I was still holding onto things that did not matter in eternity. I needed to let go and go with what God had called me to be and do.

Warren and I were leaving breakfast one morning when I told him, "Sometimes I feel like I'm out of place. I don't like the system." I'll never forget him wheeling around and pointing his finger at me.

"Michael," he said, "God uses mavericks. Jim Cymbala is a maverick. Moody was a maverick. Spurgeon was a maverick. They cut their own path. They followed God and their heart. Don't settle."

No one had ever given me permission to be a maverick before! I had watched others do it, but I wasn't sure I could. I worried too much about my security. I had to let go. I had to surrender. That morning at the conference in Tampa, Jim Cymbala preached a message just for me. I don't know who else was in the room, but I heard it loud and clear.

Later that day I went to my room to work on a sermon, and God began to work on me. I was sitting at the small desk in my room, and as I looked in the mirror, I didn't like what I saw. It was as if God was saying, "Michael, I don't like the way you are thinking and acting right now. You want to coast and not rock the boat. I called you to be a prophet and to speak the Word without apology. You are looking at the crowd, worried about their opinions. Stop it!"

The next Sunday I told the church what had happened. I was ready for God to work or for Him to release me. Either way, I wasn't going to go with the status quo anymore. I told them why we were making the changes we were making. I'm sure some of them thought I had lost my mind, but that day I drew a line in the sand. I wasn't going to back up or back down anymore.

At an evening service around this time, I called on the church moderator to come to the platform, and I asked the congregation to decide once and for all if we were willing to be the church God had called us to be no matter what the cost. The vote was unanimous. I don't think any of us realized how costly that vote would be.

Unrest Leads to Revival

One of the real turning points came in 1992. Junior Hill was scheduled to preach a one-day crusade, and four days earlier we had to dismiss a staff member for insubordination and divisiveness. He did not leave quietly. There was rumbling in the air. I had not been at Sherwood long enough to earn the total trust of the people. Some were still longing for the former pastor to return so they could get back to the good old days before "Catt stirred up the church." My wife would sit in services and overhear people criticizing me and longing for the former pastor. It was hard not to be defensive and reactionary. To be honest I caved into my flesh at times.

When we had to dismiss the staff member, I knew we were going to have trouble. The seeds he had sown started bearing fruit almost immediately. There was an undercurrent of unrest and distrust in the church. I was sure the Junior Hill event was going to be a failure.

I almost cancelled the crusade, but when I heard from Junior that God had spoken to him about trusting Him with the meeting, we went forward with it. He came that Sunday and "preached the stars down." On a day when I thought we might have a riot, we had revival. Fifty-four people came to Christ, and we baptized thirty-nine. In many ways we never looked back after that incident. God supernaturally intervened at the point of our need. He overruled what the devil had planned. Man may think he rules, but God overrules. I learned to trust God to be my strong tower in tough times.

I also had to learn to die to my reputation. There was still a part of me that wanted to be popular and famous and significant. Call it the "only child" syndrome. Call it insecurity. I just really wanted people to like me. I had to learn to die to what people say, whether positive or negative, whether flattering or flattening.

Another thing I learned was that I was called to Sherwood for the long haul, and if I was going to be long-term and not a flash in the pan, I had to slowly move the church in another direction. I couldn't turn the ship around too fast. The biggest mistake pastors and leaders make is doing too much too soon and then moving on when they can't take the heat. If you aren't willing to stay, you can't earn the credibility or trust to make the changes. Just because the sign on the door says "Pastor" doesn't mean they are going to let you be their pastor and lead them.

> *Just because the sign on the door says "Pastor" doesn't mean they are going to let you be their pastor and lead them.*

Conflict over Music Styles

We had another "back-door revival" over changes in the worship style. We were a toe-tapping, Southern Gospel, Gaither-music kind of church. There's nothing wrong with that, but our community is over sixty percent African-American. If we were going to be anything more than a white, dying church, we had to reflect the community.

So we tried out different styles of worship. Before building the new worship center, we had three different morning services. One service was traditional with nothing but hymns. The other two were blended with hymns and choruses. Unfortunately, we discovered that instead of building unity, we drew greater lines of division. When we finished the new worship center and were able to go back to one service, the two groups didn't know each other—and didn't like each other's music. All I had done was accommodate personal likes and dislikes. I had not led the church to a true understanding of worship, or helped people understand what a church is supposed to be and do.

One Sunday night I had reached the breaking point after having to listen that day to one complaint after another about the music. I don't know if it was my flesh or not, but I closed the service by taking a stand and then quoted Bob Dole who said (in response to those who questioned his leadership) "The exits are clearly marked."

Part of the congregation took me up on those words. Several hundred members left within two months and joined a church down the street. We had another exodus about that same time when one of our staff left and took a pastorate a few miles from us. About 160 adults went with him.

These "back-door revivals" took the wind out of our sails. We lost all the momentum of a new building. It was a gut punch. Every Sunday it seemed all anyone could talk about was those who had left. I got to the point where I would come into the office on Monday and ask, "Who left this week?" People from the other church were calling our members to tell them "who we got from Sherwood today." They were visiting our shut-ins and encouraging them to move their membership to a church where they would be loved. I saw how ugly and evil a competitive spirit can be in the church. It's not pretty, and God will not bless it.

I'm sad to say that it took us almost two years to recover from the last exodus. People in the community were asking, "What's wrong with Sherwood?" Even former staff and pastors were criticizing us. One former pastor told a preacher in another state, "Catt has ruined my church." I always try to pray for those who criticize us, but I have to admit that praying for them was hard. Still, my reputation is yielded to the Lord and, like Paul, I'm going to wait on God to judge the motives and methods.

The Right Thing to Do

But you know what? In the long run, these exoduses didn't hurt us. We started experiencing freedom in our worship; the antagonistic spirit was gone. We were delivered from the group who wanted to run the church according to their preferences. Did I hate to lose them? Yes. Was it the right thing to do? Looking back with hindsight, yes. We are distinctively different from any other Baptist church in our area. Our music and worship provide a viable option from the traditional course. We are attracting hundreds of young adults, singles and students. If I had to do it all over again, I would choose the same path.

We began inviting Christian bands and artists like TRUTH, 4Him, Wayne Watson and others to help us expand our musical horizons. Alicia Williamson was the first African-American to ever sing at Sherwood. She did a concert for us in the early 1990s. She is now on staff at Liberty University and travels the country teaching and singing. I caught a lot of flack for having an African-American stand on "our" stage, but she helped us break the racial barrier.

Today if you visit our services, you will find a beautiful mix of races and generations. More than a dozen nationalities and ethnic backgrounds are represented in our congregation. What if I had let the naysayers win? What if I had caved into the pressure? What if the church as a whole had not supported what I was trying to do? We wouldn't be who we are today. I enjoy seeing what God has done to move us toward being a New Testament church.

Even when I made a dumb decision, He worked it all around to His glory and for our good.

Someone said to me after one back-door purging, "Pastor, you shouldn't be upset. Every malcontent and high-maintenance troublemaker we had in this church has left. You ought to be praising God." He was right, and I am praising God. Since that last exodus I've not had one negative appointment or one anonymous letter.

As I think back through my years of ministry at Sherwood,

I realize God has been orchestrating it all. Even when I made a dumb decision, He worked it all around to His glory and for our good. I've been blessed to have wise men and older ministers who have poured their wisdom and insight into my life. They have offered discerning words of caution.

One of the key components to our being the church we are today was the ministry of Ron Dunn. Ron was another mentor, my best friend and the finest Bible teacher I've ever known. I first heard Ron preach in the 1970s, the week after his oldest son committed suicide. His book, *When Heaven Is Silent*, is the story of how God works in dark times.

Every year from 1990 until his death in 2001, Ron preached a four-day Bible conference at our church. Ron was an expositor who could bring truth to light in a way I've never seen in anyone else. He cut through the facades of religion and pretense. People began to grasp what he was saying. They saw the difference between legalism and spirit-filled living. Ron helped take our church to a deeper level of commitment and Christlikeness. Much of who we are today is because of the ministry of Ron Dunn.

When the "back-door revivals" began, Ron helped me to discern what was happening at Sherwood. He told me, "Anything that causes you to pray is a blessing." I can tell you from experience that it did, and it was. Conflict will cause you to pray. Gossip will cause you to pray.

Most of all, we survived those crises because of the prayer ministry. People have prayed for me, for the leadership and for the church. Our deacons gave incredible support and encouragement. They stood their ground like a stone wall. I've never seen men more committed to being New Testament deacons than the men at Sherwood.

The spirit in the church is the sweetest it's ever been. People are giving like they've never given before. The new people that are coming in are in love with Jesus and love the local church. We aren't seeking to build a church by transferring sheep from one pasture to another in our community. We want to reach the lost and unchurched. God is drawing people to this fellowship who want to make a difference with their lives. They are serving, witnessing and giving out of pure love for Christ.

Many if not most of the churches in my denomination are stagnant or declining. Thousands did not baptize one person last year. Millions of sermons, prayers and offerings, and yet no one was saved. Churches are divided generationally because senior saints have little energy or interest in reaching young people. Surely Christ died for more than that! I'm determined to invest my life in a church where we can leave a legacy for the next generation.

The back-door exodus at Sherwood was difficult to handle, but even worse than that was a personal giant that blind-sided me beyond all my expectations. I was totally unprepared for what happened, and to be honest, I didn't like what I saw in myself when it all started to unravel.

3

Facing My Own Giant

*M*Y WIFE and I were invited to speak at the 20th anniversary of the Christian music group TRUTH in Orlando, Florida. TRUTH had been an influential part of my life and ministry since their first year on the road, and Roger Breland, founder of the group, is one of my best friends.

Terri and I were also celebrating our wedding anniversary, so one night we decided to enjoy some Florida seafood and spend a quiet evening at a local restaurant. While we were talking over dinner, I said something to the effect of, "I sometimes wonder if I'm adopted. It makes no sense. I'm nothing like my parents." I had said this a few times before, and we joked about it because I am as different as night and day from my folks.

I will never forget what happened next as long as God gives me breath. Terri asked, "If you were adopted would you want to know it?" I thought about it for a moment and said, "Well, sure. I think so." I had no idea that she had been praying for several months for God to give her a window of opportunity to tell me something.

Over that meal Terri told me of a bizarre meeting her mother had a few months before with an elderly customer in her flower shop. The lady asked who Terri had married, so my mother-in-law told her about our family. The customer responded, "Oh, I know who Michael Catt is. His was the first adoption I handled when I moved to town as a social worker."

---------- ⌘ ----------

Anger stirred in my heart; unbelief haunted me. Thoughts of how I had been deceived ran rampant through the corridors of my mind.

Over the next few weeks, Terri and my mother-in-law contacted the lady to get more details. They discovered her story had validity. She knew facts about my family that no one would have known—information that had been hidden from me for nearly forty years.

The only problem Terri had now was how to tell me. If you love someone you don't just walk into the room and say, "Hey honey, you're adopted. What do you want for dinner?"

That discussion with my wife forced me to face a whole new giant in my life. I was shaken to the core. Anger stirred in my heart; unbelief haunted me. Thoughts of how I had been deceived ran rampant through the corridors of my mind.

I couldn't bring myself to call my aging parents and confront them. They had always talked about how I was like my grandfather who was an extrovert. My mother would warn me about sugar because "diabetes runs in our family." As I began to unpeel the onion, I found that the cover-up, in my mind, could rival Watergate. Apparently everyone knew but me. My childhood pastor and youth minister knew it. The church secretary knew it. All my Sunday school teachers knew it. My aunts, uncles and cousins knew it. I felt like I had been cut off at the knees.

When I returned to Albany, I took some time off and went to the mountains. The deacon chairman said, "Take all the time you need. We'll handle it." I find I can hear God clearly when I'm in the mountains, and I definitely needed to hear Him. Terri went with me, and we stayed there for two weeks. I pouted, sulked, cried out to God and complained to my wife. She should have received a medal of honor for bravery under fire.

I thought to myself, *I'm almost forty years old. Is this what a mid-life crisis feels like? Am I going to make it through this? How do I handle it? How do I move forward?* In the days following this discovery, my mind was flooded with all kinds of questions: *Why didn't my parents tell me? What were they scared of? What were they hiding? Who were my birth parents? Why did they give me up? Was I an ugly baby? Was I an accident or an inconvenience?*

Then my thoughts turned to the obvious: *Now what?* Nothing I could do would change the circumstances, but I needed some kind of closure. I needed answers. I needed direction. Should I confront my parents? Should I look for my birth parents? I received advice from dozens of people, most of it well-intentioned but not helpful. When people are hurting we often say too much. What hurting people want is the Word with skin on, not flowery speech. They want a hug, not a lecture.

Many people were praying. I was being lifted before the throne of grace by hundreds of people who knew I wasn't handling this well. If we hadn't started the intercessory prayer ministry, I wonder whether I would have survived that crisis of belief. Without the prayers that were offered up on my behalf, I might not have made it. When we're on top, our friends know us, but it's when we hit bottom that we know who our friends really are.

One of those who stood by me was Ron Dunn. He gave me some wise advice one night that probably helped me keep my sanity. I knew Ron had suffered trials, loss and adversity that I couldn't even imagine. He had been through valleys so deep they made mine look like a small ditch. I knew he was speaking from experience when he said, "I've been to the bottom and it's solid ground. You can trust God with this."

My longtime friend Roger Breland called me all the way from Hawaii where TRUTH was on a concert tour. He said, "God must love you a lot to allow you to be chosen twice." The conversation didn't last five minutes, but its impact continues. It was a turning point in my thinking. I wasn't over it, but I knew I would survive and be better, instead of bitter.

Letting God out of the Box

When you are young you think you have all the answers and nothing can stop you. But you'll discover that the older you get, the less you know and understand. All of us have preconceived ideas about how God works, but we find that His working cannot be dictated by our demands or expectations. We expect a fast ball, and He throws us a curve. We think we should turn left, and He leads us to the right. We pray for revival, expecting God to come in like a tidal wave, and He moves quietly like the tide. We look for a mighty rushing wind, and He speaks with a still small voice. My friend Wayne Watson wrote a song that said it all:

> Down on the corner they've got it all figured out.
> Little room for mystery, little room for doubt. . . .
> God ain't gonna stay in that little box you put Him in.[1]

God will not stay in the box of our theology or methodology. He will move to make us seek Him. At least that's what He did with me. God was destroying my "little box," working to rip things out of my life that didn't look

God was destroying my "little box," working to rip things out of my life that didn't look like Jesus.

like Jesus. I thought God was a Southern Baptist from the deep South. I learned a lot about who He really is and how He works.

When I learned I was adopted, I struggled to maintain my emotional balance so that I could still be the pastor of a church, a good husband and a good father. At the same time I found myself wondering why God was allowing this to happen. *Why this? Why now? What now?* I couldn't find God's perspective, and to be honest, I didn't see how God could get glory in it all.

Then Ron Dunn directed me to Isaiah 45. You'd think I would have gone to the Psalms or Romans 8:28, but I found refuge in the book of Isaiah. I found myself reading it, embracing it and hearing God speak to me from it. Today it is one of my favorite passages to preach from.

The chapter opens with the Lord proclaiming how He would accomplish His plans for Israel through "Cyrus, my anointed." The people of Israel must have been at least as confused about Cyrus as I was about my adoption. Cyrus was a pagan king, a godless man. How could God use someone like that? Cyrus didn't care about Israel; he had his own agenda.

But the fact remains that God used Cyrus even though Cyrus didn't have a clue. A.W. Pink wrote, "God is a law unto Himself, and . . . He is under no obligation to give an account of His matters to any."[2] There have been several times when God used a Cyrus in my life. This wasn't the first or last time, but I had never seen it so clearly.

In Isaiah 45, I was driven to the phrases "I am the LORD and there is no other" (v. 5) and "I am the LORD who does all these" (v. 7). Isaiah reiterated this thought six times in one chapter. God was in charge. God knew what was going on. God did it, allowed it and orchestrated it. Stephen Charnock wrote, "To be God and sovereign are inseparable."

Sometimes we can't imagine God working outside our box, our denomination, our theology or our system. I have to admit that it sometimes bothers me that God blesses people I disagree with. I, like the Israelites, would have to say I struggle when God uses someone like Cyrus. But He isn't bound by my thoughts about how He should work. It bothers me that God uses problems to perfect us. It would be so much easier if he would just zap us with microwave spirituality. I would certainly never vote for God to use a Cyrus. I would never call Cyrus "God's anointed." I had to learn that God is in charge and I'm not—or, as Martin Luther put it, "Let God be God!" Embracing those four words would revolutionize the way we view life and circumstances beyond our control.

And so, I have resigned as CEO of my life. I've lost control. It is frightening and yet fulfilling. God doesn't ask for my vote or my opinion. He certainly didn't consult me about the timing of the test of my adoption. My answer would have been "No!" I would have run from it kicking and screaming. Today I embrace it as part of God's perfect will for my life. I can now agree with Matthew Henry who said, "Sanctified afflictions are spiritual promotions."

Sometimes when I'm speaking at a Bible conference, I'll preach on Isaiah 45 and mention the story of my adoption. Rarely do I share that story without someone coming up to me and telling me a similar one. Knowing that I've survived this setback seems to encourage them. The devil wants us to focus on the giants, but God uses those giants to bring us back to focus on Him.

Learning to forgive my parents for keeping the truth from me was a process. I had to realize that things were different in the 1950s; people just didn't talk about adoption. It doesn't explain all their reasoning, but it helps. It was never fully resolved, but I have fully forgiven any intended or unintended deception based on fear or insecurity. By God's sovereign plan I was adopted by Christian parents who made sure I was in church. They weren't perfect, but they did love me.

I've learned to thank God for a young airline stewardess who got pregnant and decided not to get a back-alley abortion. I know about her, although I've never met her. I have no idea who my birth father is. I've been told he was a Marine. There are some things that will only be understood in eternity. As Warren Wiersbe writes, "People live by promises, not by explanations. God is not standing at the end of a syllogism, nor is peace of mind found at the conclusion of an argument. In every area of life there must be an element of faith."[3] I know this: I am here by the grace of God, for the purpose of God, to live my life to the glory of God.

God wanted me to go deeper. He was taking me back to promises I had made when I was first saved.

Today, nearly fifteen years later, I see how God used this faith crisis to mold me more and more into His image. It has given me a greater appreciation of my spiritual adoption, as pointed out in a quote I read by John Murray: "Adoption, as the term clearly implies, is an act of transfer from an alien family into the family of God Himself. This is surely the apex of grace and privilege."[4]

I've learned more from my defeats than my victories. I've discovered more about who God is from my trials than my triumphs. Fire is the test of gold; adversity is the test of strong men. Pruning is painful but necessary if we want to bear fruit. I was too full of myself. I operated too much in the flesh. God needed to get my attention, and He certainly did.

God wanted me to go deeper. He was taking me back to promises I had made when I was first saved. He longed for me to have a greater understanding of His sovereignty. I needed to abide if I was going to abound. I had preached it, but now I was forced to live it. I had begun to learn what Charles Spurgeon meant when he wrote, "In shunning a trial we are seeking to avoid a blessing."[5]

Think about Job, who stayed true and never cursed God throughout all his afflictions. If he had, we wouldn't blame him, but we wouldn't remember him either. God never told him why all these things happened. Job had his struggle, but in the last few chapters of the book of Job, you find a man who knew God in ways most of us will never understand.

Paul never got an answer for his thorn in the flesh; what he did get was grace that was sufficient. If John Bunyan hadn't been in prison, he might have never written *Pilgrim's Progress.* The saints of old and many of the heroes of the church went through battles, and their lives are a blessing to us today. That's why when situations, crises and conflicts come in our lives, we need to accept them rather than complain about *what* God is doing, *who* He is using to prune us or *how* He is working. Just because we can't see all that God is doing doesn't mean we have a right to complain about it.

In Genesis when Joseph was speaking to his brothers about all that had happened, six times he said, "You meant it for evil, but God meant it for good." Ron Dunn used to say, "Only God can take our setbacks and turn them into our salvation." Satan wanted to use the revelation of my adoption to cut me down. God used it to prune me. Satan wanted to destroy me inside. God wanted to take me deeper.

Whatever your personal battle may be, God is in control. Even if God is using a "Cyrus" in your life, remember: He is the Lord, and there is no other. If God can hold the stars in their place, He can hold you in the palm of His hand. His grace is sufficient. God loves the weak, and His heart is compassionate toward desperate people. Trace it through the Scriptures. When people get desperate, they always seem to find God. Or maybe it's that God reaches them.

Moses in the wilderness; Jonah in the fish; Elijah by the brook; Jeremiah in the pit; blind Bartimaeus on the roadside; the woman with the issue of blood; the centurion and a hundred others—all had one thing in common: an overwhelming giant in their lives. They were desperate, and God met them where they were. Be where you are supposed to be, when you are supposed to be there, doing what you are supposed to be doing, and the Lord God of heaven will meet you there.

We All Face Giants

I can really relate to the man who came to Jesus and said, "Lord, I believe. Help my unbelief!" (Mark 9:24). I believe God can do anything, but there are days when I need help with my unbelief. When you encounter things that are insurmountable, it can lead you to a crisis of faith. The good news, however, is that God is attracted to weak and desperate people.

Every believer, at some time in life, reaches

All of us, if we are honest with ourselves, will admit to having skeletons in the closet—issues that we try to hide or deny, issues that cause us to question the love of God or our worth as believers.

a point of weakness and desperation. All of us, if we are honest with ourselves, will admit to having skeletons in the closet—issues that we try to hide or deny, issues that cause us to question the love of God or our worth as believers. They can loom as large as giants, taunting us and cursing us, just like Goliath did to the armies of Israel.

Those who grew up in homes without Christian love or guidance will find that it breeds many giants in their lives. They may wonder if God the Father loves them, especially if they did not have a loving earthly father. This is an issue the church will increasingly have to deal with in light of the number of children raised in broken homes in America.

For some it is the lack of children that is the giant in their lives. Early in our marriage Terri and I dealt with the issue of infertility. While our friends were all having babies, our nursery remained empty. We went through all the embarrassing tests and exams to see what or who might be the problem. We tried for years with no success. We prayed, claimed Scripture and asked others to join us in prayer, but nothing happened.

In the early 1980s we began to think about adoption. As we began the process, I got a call from a friend in another state. A member of his church had a teenage daughter who was pregnant out of wedlock. We began working on the details of getting a lawyer and making that baby ours. Six months into her pregnancy, the young girl's older sister paid for her to have an abortion. I can't begin to tell you how that hurt. We were so close, yet so far.

Just when we were becoming discouraged, God gave us a clear promise out of the Psalms which we held onto for exactly five years: "He makes the barren woman abide in the house as the joyful mother of children. Praise the Lord!" (Ps. 113:9, NASB). At five years to the month from when we first started trying to have children, Terri became pregnant. God has given us two beautiful, godly girls, Erin and Hayley. What a blessing they are to our lives! We know they are God's gifts to us. Even though they are adults now, I can't look at them without thinking of God's gracious provision when all seemed hopeless.

Health concerns can become a giant in our lives as well. Alex and Stephen Kendrick, our staff members who wrote and directed *Facing the Giants*, have watched their father Larry face giants of his own. In fact, the character of Larry Childers in *Facing the Giants* is patterned after their dad. In 1984 Larry was diagnosed with multiple sclerosis, and in the months that followed, he began to spiral into a pit of depression. He struggled spiritually and emotionally to understand what God was doing while he battled severe numbness and burning pain physically.

Larry finally hit rock bottom and cried out to the Lord through tears of desperation. "Jesus, even though I do not understand, I will praise you whether you heal me or not. I will not walk away from you!" When he could have given up and turned away, he continued to serve the Lord faithfully and honor God with his life. He remained a solid example to his wife and sons.

Since that diagnosis, Larry Kendrick has founded Cumberland Christian Academy in the Atlanta area. God has blessed this man's faithfulness and perseverance. As a result, Alex and Stephen have a legacy of trusting God for the impossible and of praising Him regardless of the circumstances. Alex and Stephen have often said that even though their dad cannot stand up physically, he stands in prayer over their lives as they serve the Lord.

Sandra Powell, the wife of one of our staff members, also has multiple sclerosis. She is one of our greatest prayer warriors. Although we've watched her decline in health, her faith in God has never wavered. She is an inspiration to the thousands of people she has written prayer cards to, and is one of the kindest and godliest people I've ever known.

We've walked through the valleys with families who have been faced with terminal cancer. We've watched young moms die of cancer, leaving behind a husband and children. I remember visiting one man with cancer who had received over 2,500 prayer cards from our intercessory prayer ministry. Although we interceded, God didn't answer the prayers the way we wanted Him to. We still believe God and trust that He is good and faithful.

Richard Vickers, one of our deacons, died of brain cancer. I was there with about twenty church members before they took him into surgery. While we were praying he was praising Jesus. One of the last times Richard was able to come to church, I looked over and saw him lifting his hands in praise to God with tears rolling down his face.

Most of us have lost family and friends to this frightening disease. It's hard to know what to say or how to pray when the doctors give you no hope. It's hard to know how to pray when people you love are diagnosed with life-threatening diseases. We've seen God intervene in miraculous ways at times, but we've also learned that God doesn't heal just because we want Him to. He does whatever will bring Him the most glory.

Setbacks seem insurmountable sometimes. Because Albany is a mid-sized city in a rural part of southwest Georgia, we've had to deal with factories and businesses closing. To see godly, active, supportive members be relocated out of our city and church is never easy. Corporate America has often impacted families and communities in ways that destroy our traditional values and leave us with unanswered questions.

We are a declining and transitional city. People come and go at an unusually high rate for a mid-sized town. People may grow up in Albany and then struggle to find jobs here after they graduate. Some of our members are Marines and are only here for two or three years. Just about the time they get plugged into the church, they get transferred. Rather than consider this a negative, we've asked God to help us train up soldiers for God's army to go around the world. The stories of what God is doing through them is a constant reminder that we are to seize the moments God gives us. When I get an email from Iraq or Japan or the Philippines, I know we made a difference in that soldier's life.

---------------- ⤳ ----------------

What is your giant?
What obstacle is blocking
your vision of God?

What is your giant? What obstacle is blocking your vision of God? It could be a person, a committee, a family member, health, finances or a thousand other things. In Mark 11 there is a great truth about seeing God above the situations of life.

In this passage Jesus came upon a fig tree that had leaves but no fruit. Jesus cursed the tree and went on His way. The following day He and the disciples passed by that fig tree again, and Simon Peter expressed surprise that the fig tree was now withered up. Simon Peter had seen all the miracles, he had walked on water, and yet he was amazed by a fig tree. Jesus' response was, in essence, "Don't be surprised by miracles."

If God can save us in our sinful condition, He can certainly meet us at the point of our need. It is the object of our faith that is crucial. We don't need bigger faith; we have a big God. God can move any obstacle that stands in our way. Jesus did not say, "When you see an immovable object, get out the jackhammers and the bulldozers." He said, "Call in the prayer warriors."

We can't take the visible as the last word. We must prepare to simply receive what God has for us. He wants us to understand how great His plans are for us, how mighty His hand is on our behalf and how awesome His power is. He is just waiting for us to step out in faith and prove Him right.

Without the intercessory prayers offered up for me and for others in our congregation, I don't think we could have had the courage to step out and face some of our giants. But God was awakening us to prayer.

4

An Environment of Prayer

*R*EGARDLESS of where we live, ministry isn't easy. We live in a postmodern world. Our churches are filled with people who have lost their commitment to absolute truth. The world is influencing the church more than the church is influencing the world. And yet, as a church we must do ministry the old-fashioned way—through prayer and hard work.

In my home church, Calvary Baptist in Pascagoula, Mississippi, a renewed emphasis on prayer was one of the many effects of the "Jesus Movement" in the 1970s. My youth pastor, James Miller, started a youth prayer ministry on Tuesday and Thursday nights.

I was at the first prayer meeting with five others, including my youth pastor and my twelfth-grade Sunday school director. In a week or so, the gathering had grown to eight, then twelve, and before long we had twenty-five to thirty. Within a matter of months, the prayer meeting had grown to well over one hundred. There was no preaching. We had one guy with a guitar who knew about three songs and would lead us in musical worship. Often we would start at 7:30 p.m. and pray until 2 a.m.

Sometimes the Spirit of God was so powerful in that place that high school students driving by the church would stop because they saw a friend's car. They would come in and immediately fall under the Holy Spirit's conviction. I saw people set free from drug, alcohol and tobacco abuse. I distinctively remember one girl who was a cheerleader in our high school. She walked in the back door and didn't make it six feet before falling on her knees and crying out, "Can somebody tell me how to be saved?" Over the next few years, that prayer meeting would have as many as 300 people in attendance. The ripples of revival through the "Jesus Movement," coupled with those prayer gatherings, marked me personally and my ministry.

I fear the missing ingredient in most churches today is prayer. Without prayer people cannot experience revival. Without prayer a church cannot survive making changes. Without prayer there cannot be unity in the church. In a prayer environment God can make the impossible possible. With this in mind we started the intercessory prayer ministry at Sherwood.

Awakened to Prayer

As a pastor my heart told me that if we were going to build buildings, get out of the box, have a vision for the region and increase our ministry impact, the first thing we had to do was pray. We had to build a praying church first. We couldn't just do ministry, tack a prayer on the end of it and expect God to bless it. We needed prayer at the forefront of all we did.

As we began our intercessory prayer ministry in 1990, people were awakened to the necessity of prayer in the church. We were a membership tired of tradition and rules. What we wanted was the power of the Holy Spirit and to see God-sized answers to our prayers.

Like most churches we had prayer meeting, but it was mostly an "organ" recital. You know the drill: pray for ingrown toenails, minor surgeries, a few big surgeries, the sick and afflicted, shut-ins and those for whom it is our duty to pray. Most of prayer meeting was focused on physically sick folks.

Now there is nothing wrong with praying for the sick. But if we are honest, we must admit we do very little praying in our churches for the spiritually sick, the prodigals and the wayward. If the church is going to be a New Testament church, she has to learn to get hold of God for impossible situations. She must learn to intercede. We can't just talk about prayer and read about prayer; we have to pray. Andrew Bonar wrote, "God likes to see His people shut up to this, that there is no hope but in prayer. Herein lies the church's power against the world."[1]

Soon we began to build a small prayer chapel on our property. A man in the church who was dying of cancer designed it. The prayer chapel was built by volunteers and was located just outside my office window. It was encouraging to sit in my office and see members coming hour after hour to pray.

The room in the prayer chapel was organized so that you could agonize. There was a prayer rail for kneeling, an old church pew and a couple of chairs. We had a desk where people could write prayer cards to those they were praying for. Since its inception we've averaged sending close to 600 prayer cards a week out of our intercessory prayer ministry. They have been sent across the street and around the world. We want to be burdened by what burdens the heart of God.

The prayer ministry is the heartbeat of who we are as a church. If it weren't for the prayer ministry, the rest of this book would be little more than flesh-peddling and bragging about who we are. Because of the prayer ministry, Sherwood is a testimony of what God can do. The secret to touching the world is to know the secret of touching the heart of God.

When we fail to pray, we disappoint Christ, defeat ourselves and delight the devil. No Christ-honoring church or ministry ever rises above the level of praying done for it.

No Christ-honoring church or ministry ever rises above the level of praying done for it.

One idea we had was to call every listing in the phone book and pray for them by name. It takes us about three years to call through all the names in our local phone book. Church members use their cell phones, home phones and office phones to call page after page of names. The testimonies of how God has used this small effort have been incredible.

While calling we've discovered dozens of unchurched people who are facing surgery. Once we called a lady who had just learned that her best friend had committed suicide. We spoke with a man who had just been served with divorce papers from his wife. We've called individuals who have had recent deaths in their families. One year we discovered over twenty people who were having surgery the next week and had no church home. We were there to pray with them. We've talked and prayed with people struggling to survive. Rarely do they tell us they don't want us to pray for them. People who are hurting need someone who cares. People who are overwhelmed by life's problems need to know someone else has been there.

> *People who are hurting need someone who cares. People who are overwhelmed by life's problems need to know someone else has been there.*

Guidance through Prayer

For the first several years after I came to Sherwood, we had issues at our Christian school. The school had been started in the 1980s by the former pastor, and people were divided over whether or not we should have it. Some were wholehearted supporters, a few were ambivalent, and others were against having it.

For a number of years, that school was my biggest headache. It seemed every day we had a problem with something or someone. There were many days I was ready to call the whole thing off. Like everything else, the school needed strong, godly leadership. We had people working at the school who were not committed members of a church and did not respect pastoral authority.

In the 1990s John Hemken was the executive pastor at Sherwood, and he and I had a running line—"Could this be the day?"—the day we don't get a call from someone complaining about some issue at the school. We didn't see that day for several years, and it seemed it would never come.

In 1994 we had an opportunity to take over the buildings and land from another private school that was going under financially. We bathed the decision in prayer. I called together a group of leaders to pray about whether or not we should take the matter to the church. They prayed for thirty days. I asked them to listen to Ron Dunn's message on knowing God's will from Romans chapter twelve and not to speak to anyone about this but the Lord. After thirty days, the answer was a unanimous "no." It was a good deal, but not a God-deal.

Several months later the board of that school contacted us again. They were willing to let us purchase their facilities and property by merely paying the debt they owed. What had been a good deal the first time had now become a great deal. We didn't rush into the decision; we prayed through it again. This time it was a unanimous "yes." We learned that the right thing at the wrong time is the wrong thing. Mountain-moving faith operates in God's timing, not ours.

The decision was taken to the deacons, and they voted in favor of it unanimously. The church members asked a few questions, then voted to buy the property with a 99.5% vote. This was a huge change in attitude—truly an answer to prayer. Our people viewed the school as a ministry of the church. It wasn't the pastor's school; it was an integral part of Sherwood's mission, vision and purpose. We purchased the seventeen-acre property, all the facilities, desks, a football field, a softball field, a gym and a cafeteria for less than $450,000. That was a God-sized answer to prayer.

Today Sherwood Christian Academy operates on two

different campuses separate from our church, but we are one in ministry. Our headmaster, Glen Schultz, headed the Christian education division of LifeWay for several years. Glen wrote the book *Kingdom Education,* which is the model for how we do ministry through the school, church and home. Today the school is a blessing and not a burden.

Prayer Is Our Lifeline

Too often we do everything but pray. We build, budget, promote, advertise, market, blog, connect, network, program and plan— but we don't pray. Prayer is the litmus test for a church. You won't ever find a church that is praying too much, but you can find one on nearly every corner that is prayerless and powerless. We promise something to a lost and dying world that we aren't producing. We're losing the next generation. Absolute truth has been replaced by relative thinking and overrun by technology. We have programs but lack power.

> *The lifeline of a church is the prayer line. We don't need smarter people or more money as much as we need people who pray.*

Miracles don't come out of methods; they come out of the context of prayer and faith. The life of a Christian is the life of prayer. The lifeline of a church is the prayer line. We don't need smarter people or more money as much as we need people who will pray.

God, and God alone, is our source for the power and authority to move mountains, make changes and build the kingdom. Faith sees God, and God sees faith. Faith is nothing more or less than believing and obeying what God says.

Ignatius wrote, "Give me men who are wholly surrendered to God, and I will convert the world with them." Few understand what God could do if they would yield themselves entirely to Him. As God's people, let's rise to believe and not doubt. Jesus is saying, "Don't ever stop trusting God. Get your eyes off the problem and get them on God." We can get lost in the culture wars and overwhelmed by the carnal condition of the church. We can immerse ourselves in canned programs, or we can turn to God and find the divine design for our ministry.

Faith is never greater than its object. We sometimes find ourselves trusting a god we've created in our own image, but faith has value when it links us to the omnipotent Lord God of heaven. Anything less won't get us where we need to be. We must trust the I AM of the Word. He, and He alone, can move mountains. A. W. Tozer said, "Faith rests upon the character of God, not upon the demonstration of laboratory or logic."[2]

What mountains are you facing? Are you a walking witness of the presence of the Holy Spirit? What we all need is power, not performance. We need to be desperate enough to believe God for the impossible. That kind of power only comes in a prayer environment.

Most of us would probably like to have the faith of a man like George Müeller. Few of us, however, want to be put in a desperate position that *demands* we trust God like George Müeller did. Are we willing to say, "Either we get it right, or we die"? Could we ever be so bold as to believe that God is bigger than the mountain? Are we a people longing for the God of the Red Sea, Jonah's great fish, the sun standing still and Pentecostal power?

Have we ruled out the supernatural because it doesn't fit our experience? Are our mountains of laws and regulations so big that they block God? Do we have mountains of doubt, insecurity, anxiety and the sins of our past that haunt us to the point where we can't see God?

With the cross in view, the mountains come into proper perspective. If I am "cross-eyed" in my spiritual vision, nothing in heaven, hell or on earth can prevent me from accomplishing God's purposes for my life. Obstacles will come. Mountains of opposition may always be there, but my focus must be on the cross, not on the mountains. In prayer, I keep a perspective I can't have any other way. In prayer, changes can be made with holy boldness. Then, when it's time to step out in faith, we have confidence in the omniscient, omnipresent, omnipotent God of glory. It's not up to me to work it out; it's up to Him to move the mountains. I don't need to consult a committee; I need to commit to Christ.

You will have doubts; you can't stop them from entering your mind. But how do you deal with them? Ron Dunn said, "You may consider the problem, but you don't take the problem into consideration."[3] The doubts may enter, but you don't have to entertain them. Don't ignore the problems, but don't dwell on them either. Doubt your doubts and trust in God.

Are you facing an insurmountable problem right now? Is there a giant in your life? Is your past defeating or discouraging you? Are you weary in well-doing? Have you forgotten the greatness of our God? Lift up your eyes and see the cross. Charles Spurgeon said, "To live by faith is a far surer and happier thing than to live by feelings or by works."[4]

In a dying community with major industries closing and people transferring out, we are seeing the hand of God. Our mountains have become minuscule. Our God is the biggest thing in our vision. He can do exceedingly abundantly beyond what we ever hoped or imagined. We want to be a church where God can be God, and we need to be people who let God be God. The best environment for that to happen is a prayer environment.

Prayer time before the Hollywood premiere of *Facing the Giants*

5

A Visionary Team

*W*ALT DISNEY said, "Think beyond your lifetime if you want to do something truly great." One day during a planning meeting at the Disney studios, Walt became irritated with his team. He said, "The trouble is you aren't thinking far enough ahead! We're just beginning! You have to think beyond Disney World! We haven't even begun to think big."[1]

In order to think big, you need to have vision, and it's impossible to separate vision from leadership. Beyond that, it's impossible to separate leadership from teamwork. There are no "lone rangers" in effective ministry. All of us need people who will stretch us. If we want to leave a legacy the next generation can be proud of, we have to build a visionary team that lays a foundation that will stand the test of time.

Through the years God has blessed us with a great staff at Sherwood. While I have a few regrets and have made some wrong choices, for the most part God has blessed us with wonderful staff. Many of them were either raised in the church or were actively involved in the church before leaving the corporate world and coming to serve at Sherwood. We've also found some incredible people in other churches who want to be a part of the vision God has given us.

Today we have a staff of thirty-seven including fourteen ordained ministers. When I first came to Sherwood, the church was down to two ordained ministers and four secretaries. The two associate pastors had done a good job of holding things together, but there was no doubt the church was understaffed. I had the privilege and responsibility of building a ministry team, but it had to be done quickly. We immediately went to work to get fully staffed.

Call it my inexperience and immaturity, or my desire to fill the positions quickly, but whatever it was, we missed it with a couple of staff members. In those early years I acted in haste. I went with my heart and forgot to use my head. I forgot the rule of "Hire slow, fire fast." No matter what the issue, letting someone go is never fun.

It's especially painful when the staff member you have to let go is a personal friend, and I've had that dubious privilege a few times. I had envisioned us serving together, but it didn't work out for one reason or another. A pastor can have friends on his staff, but you have to be careful not to confuse roles and relationships. Friendship doesn't automatically insure that a person is the right fit for a particular position. Building a team is, to me, the toughest part of the job.

When I first became a pastor, I asked for an appointment with one of the leading pastors in my denomination. I asked him what my number one problem would be as a pastor. He said, "Ninety-five percent of your problems will be staff related. The guy in the back row won't be the one that stirs up the church. It will be a dissatisfied or unqualified staff member that doesn't do what he is supposed to do." I jotted that thought down, but I didn't know I'd have to live it out.

There is nothing more painful than dealing with staff issues. You enter the relationship with high hopes. You put your reputation on the line to bring them before the church. The church embraces them, pays them and loves them. But if you get one with his own agenda, problems abound and little gets done for the kingdom. For a leadership team to work, everyone has to be on the same page. They have to work within the overall vision of the church. A church cannot move forward with leadership or laity that has any other agenda than the glory of God.

Superstars Need Not Apply

It's tough to build a team, and like I said, we made a few mistakes in looking for new team members. Some staff people hit a limit in their thinking and can't see or envision on the scale you hope they can. Others want to get the credit and resist an environment where there are no superstars, just servants.

Some people in ministry seem content to draw a paycheck and drink coffee with the good ol' boys. Some seem to be in ministry for themselves. It doesn't work! It takes a team of *servant-hearted* people to accomplish life-changing ministry. You can't think out-

Many churches spend more energy discussing what they can't do than praying about what they could do.

side the box if you surround yourself with cookie-cutter thinkers. Many churches spend more energy discussing what they can't do than praying about what they could do.

A senior pastor needs next-level thinkers on his team—people who ask, "What if . . . ?" You need players, not pretenders. You need people who can be counted on to show up every day and give their all for the cause of Christ. We prayed for a team that would dream big. Little did I know when I asked God for that kind of staff that they would stretch me to the limit!

The Sherwood team is the best I've ever known. They do their jobs and allow me to do mine. I'm called as a pastor to pray and preach the Word. My responsibility is to get the right players on the field and then release them to do their jobs within the context of our vision, mission and purpose.

Some think building a team is impossible. How do you do it in this day of egos and superstars? We know the pastor's name, but few know the names of the people behind the scenes. Paul was never afraid to give credit to his team. He knew their importance. He was able to accomplish all he did because of men like Silas, Timothy and Luke. Imagine if Paul hadn't had a physician with him like Luke. He might have never recovered from his many beatings. Paul was willing to give credit where credit was due.

If you watch much religious television, you have to wonder what the church did before cable and satellite. Some today consider themselves God's gift to the church. You'll be successful if you read their book. You'll have money if you pad their pockets. There's more strutting on religious television today than you'll find in a whole barnyard of roosters!

It's funny how name-driven many TV ministries seem to

be. I can name the pastors of a dozen churches that have national television ministries, but most viewers don't have a clue what the name of the church is or where it's located. The 21st-century church smacks of ego in such a way that it's no wonder the world rejects us.

> *The 21st-century smacks of ego in such a way that it's no wonder the world rejects us.*

It is said that P.T. Barnum invited Charles Spurgeon to preach at his circus in America and offered to pay him a significant amount of money. Spurgeon declined politely and wrote "Acts 13:10" next to his signature, which read: "O full of all deceit and all fraud, you son of the devil, you enemy of all righteousness, will you not cease perverting the straight ways of the Lord?"[2] In this day of success, marketing, showmanship and high-tech gadgetry, no one would turn down an offer like that—and certainly not with such language! But then, there are no Spurgeons on television either.

A Good Staff Is Priceless

Because I spent the first fifteen years in ministry serving as a staff member, I know the value of a strong team. A pastor is only as strong as the people he surrounds himself with. He needs to continually recognize the individual contributions of the team and give appropriate praise. As John Maxwell often says in his conferences, "teamwork makes the dream work."

It's amazing what can be done when you don't care who gets the recognition. As a staff member and a pastor, I understood that most positions are not highly visible. If you aren't the senior pastor, minister of music or the person reading the announcements, you rarely get the pulpit. I also know that jockeying for position is never the path to success in the ministry. God knows where you are, and when He needs you He will call. You have to let go of your ego to be effective on a church staff or other team.

While staff members may have different levels of responsibility, there are no staff positions or ministries more important than another. If we didn't have good secretaries and administrative assistants, we couldn't function like we do.

We are all called to serve. Despite the success of this ministry and the movies we've produced, there are no celebrities on our team. Some serve in more visible capacities, but all are part of the same body. If we are working with one purpose—the glory of God—the possibilities are endless.

This may seem counter-cultural, as success has become more about networking, marketing and parading our successes. The church has developed a corporate mentality with a focus on being seen in the spotlight. But if we are called of God, we can't get stressed out about getting enough "platform time." Leaders need to lead, but their leadership has to be centered on others.

I've seen the success and celebrity syndrome kill a ministry. It can easily happen with talented people when they develop a "They're lucky to have me" attitude. I once served with a minister of music who was constantly in a knot about "his time" and "my time" in the worship service. He apparently had been taught in college that the minister of music is the worship leader, when in reality, he should be working with and under the pastor's leadership. If the pastor isn't giving his input into how the service should flow, he's not being the leader. Worship is not about platform time; it's about the Lord. If worship becomes a "my time" versus "your time" scenario, God is not going to show up.

The same thing applies to Christian artists who demand the spotlight and the stage. Roger Breland, the director of TRUTH, told me that over the group's twenty years of ministry he had to take some very gifted people aside and remind them, "It's not about you!" Dying to self is essential if you are going to have a team approach to ministry. There's no room for egos or agendas if we are doing Kingdom business.

The "What's in it for me?" attitude can kill a church or ministry. It's easy to become more concerned about titles than ministry. In the early 1990s my executive pastor was constantly dealing with a couple of staff members who seemed to be obsessed with who was getting the most time with the pastor. It sounded, looked and smelled a lot like James and John asking for the power seats next to Jesus in His kingdom. In hindsight we probably put up with that attitude too long. We were trying to work through the situation, but we really needed to part ways and move on. If someone is more concerned about being in the inner circle than ministering to people, the results can be disastrous.

Other things we look for in staff members are strong families and healthy marriages. No one is perfect, but if it's not right at home, it won't be right at church. Howard Hendricks said once: "If it's not working at home, don't export it." We are as concerned about the staff member's spouse and kids as we are about the staff member himself.

We don't "hire" spouses, but we need to make sure they believe in their partners' ministry. We want them to be excited about being at Sherwood. If they come along kicking and screaming, you can count on trouble down the road. I know this: A man's wife is a reflection of his spiritual leadership (or lack of it) in his home.

Finding the Right Fit

Building a staff is like buying a pair of shoes. One size doesn't fit all, and if you don't choose the right pair, you'll get blisters. If you don't have the right team in leadership positions, it's going to rub some people the wrong way. You can find people to plug holes, but finding the person who can empower others to do the work of ministry is a different ball game.

On a few occasions the personalities didn't gel with our team. A couple of times the résumé looked great and the recommendations were strong, but I think someone was just trying to unload their problem on another church.

There have been occasions when we missed it and called the wrong person. These situations are stressful and demand immediate action. The pastor's responsibility is to protect the flock, and if there's a problem it needs to be dealt with.

It's easy to get excited about coming to a new position or a new church, but it's not how high you jump; it's how straight you walk when you land. The real test of a minister's character is in how he leaves when that day comes. Through thirty-five years of ministry, I've watched several walk out like godly men, while others left seemingly bent on destroying the church as much as possible on their way out. They've emptied their guns, shooting over their shoulders as they've left. People who do this have little regard for the bloodied bodies they leave on the field as they applaud themselves for their carnal actions. Somewhere along the line, they forget it's God's church.

Christians are like sheep among wolves, but you have to be aware of wolves wearing sheep skins. There is no room for wolves in God's flock, and there's no room for hirelings in the Lord's ministry. Had it not been for the Lord and the prayers of godly people, we would not have survived those conflicts.

We all know there are two sides to a story. I've been fired twice in my ministry. In one case I wasn't given a dime and was cut off immediately. In the other, I got two weeks pay and that was it. After those experiences I want to take the high road whenever possible because I know the sting of failure. Even if a person doesn't fit our team, I want to do the right thing, and sometimes no matter what you do, it's not enough. One friend said to me, "It seems that those you do the most for are never satisfied," and I've found that to be true at times.

If you do reach an impasse, it's still important to be Christlike when you let someone go. I've rarely told the church why we dismissed a staff member, because the truth doesn't need defending, and I don't want to get into a "he said/they said" situation. God is the ultimate Judge. He's the One who will balance the books one day. My job is to protect the church and move on. I have to insure we are united in our mission, purpose and vision.

Although some of our team have left us wounded, I try to keep the lines of communication open. I can't determine how someone else will act, but I can do what's right. Some of them don't know it, but I've recommended them to their present positions where they are serving and being used of God.

Paul and Barnabas had a dispute regarding their team. On the second missionary journey, Barnabas wanted to take John Mark with them. Paul disagreed, remembering the sting he felt when John Mark left them in the middle of the first missionary journey. I believe you can accurately say that Paul and Barnabas had a falling out. They continued to minister but went in two different directions.

Years later Paul wrote to Timothy and asked him to come and bring John Mark with him. Apparently Barnabas (and possibly Peter) had taken the young disciple and invested in his life. John Mark had learned from his mistakes. He wasn't bitter at Paul for the tough decision not to let him join his staff on the second journey. Paul now said, "He is useful to me for ministry."

Even Paul made decisions where he later changed his mind. No leader is perfect, and no one gets it right every time. The issue is the heart. What's your motive in having a team? Why do you need them? What do you look for in a team?

First of all you need people who share your vision. It's not easy to get staff members to move to Albany, Georgia. It's not the hot spot on the map. It's a dying community and lacking in things to do outside the church. But it's a beautiful city, and we always hope we can call a staff member when the azaleas and dogwoods are blooming.

Secondly, you have to cast the vision. It's more than buildings and budgets. It's about a vision that can impact people for eternity. Our vision is to touch the world from Albany, Georgia. That's not an easy sell. Whoever heard of a small town touching the world? One day God reminded me that nothing much happened in Bethlehem until Jesus showed up. In fact, about all you read of Bethlehem in the Old Testament is that it's the place where Rachel died. A place of death became a place of life. That's what we want this church to be—light and life in a dark and decaying society.

Thirdly, you have to see the team as a whole. You need the right mix. Not everyone needs to be an upfront person. You need "behind the scenes" players who put their hands to the plow and do their jobs with excellence. You need people with expertise who can fill the gaps.

> *We all have strengths and weaknesses. We need to play to our strengths and we need others around us who can cover for our weaknesses.*

We all have strengths and weaknesses. We need to play to our strengths, and we need others around us who can cover for our weaknesses. If all of the disciples had been like Simon Peter, no one could have been the leader. It takes the quiet disciples as well as the outspoken ones to make a team that impacts the world.

In Matthew 10:1 we read, "He called His twelve disciples to Him and gave them authority." Notice what Jesus did: He delegated authority. He empowered them to act as His disciples because they would represent Him to the people. He then equipped them with the tools they needed to get the job done. Our Lord Jesus set the example for us. He used a team to multiply ministry.

If any one man could do it all, it was Jesus, but He chose to use a team. Personally, I need a team. I love a team environment. I consider our staff mighty men of valor. They are men who will go the second mile and do whatever it takes to get the job done. We don't have any narrow thinkers on this team. They are constantly thinking, stretching, imagining and dreaming about what God might do next in this place. I hope they all buy burial plots and spend the rest of their ministry here!

Great teams are others-centered. Great teams recognize the laity. Great team players partner with one another to get the task done. To paraphrase John Wooden, one man may shoot the ball, but it took four other sets of hands to get him in that position. When one wins, we all win.

For Sherwood, much of our attention has come through Sherwood Pictures, our television ministry, our sports and recreation ministry or the ReFRESH Conferences (conferences designed to renew and refresh church leaders). But if we weren't doing the basics well with Bible study, children, youth, Sherwood Christian Academy and our other ministries, the church could not flourish.

Right now we're getting an unusual amount of attention for *Facing the Giants*. I will say without reservation that if this team were not willing to pull together and cheer for one another, the movie would have never been made. Staff members were willing to pick up the slack for those who were actively involved in the movie. The staff members have been the biggest cheerleaders for one another. This staff knows when one wins we all win.

The story is told that in the latter part of the 19th century, when a church denomination was holding its annual convention, one leader stood up to share his vision for the church and missions. He began to talk about how he believed one day men would be able to fly from place to place to share the gospel.

Another leader, Bishop Wright, retorted disdainfully, "Heresy! Flight is reserved for the angels." After the conference, the bishop returned home with his two sons, Orville and Wilbur. That's right—a few years later on December 17, 1903, the sons of the protestor did what their father said was impossible.[3]

I've spent all my life hearing people tell me why we can't do something. I refuse to let negative people determine the destiny of the church. I've watched our team energize, agonize for and support one another. The staff of Sherwood inspires me to work harder, preach better, dream bigger and love more. They are truly a visionary team.

Groundbreaking ceremony for the new sports park

6

Attitude Is Everything

$\mathcal{I}$N THE MOVIE *Facing the Giants*, football coach Grant Taylor asks his team what their purpose is. He gets a variety of answers, and most of them are not what he's looking for. Then he challenges his team to play for the glory of God. "If we win, we praise Him. If we lose, we praise Him. Either way, we give God our best."

When I think of Sherwood today, I am reminded of that scene in the movie—and also of Paul's opening words in his first letter to the church at Thessalonica. He commended these believers for their faithfulness, love, steadfast hope and spiritual power, making them an example to Christians all over the world.

Who wouldn't want to be in a church like that? They were both famous and faithful. Some churches are famous, but when you examine them they are a mile wide and an inch deep. God's evaluation of the Thessalonian church was that it was healthy overall.

≈

Not all large churches are healthy. A healthy church is one that brings glory to God through its godly attitudes.

In America, however, it seems we only measure a church by size. I heard something a Russian pastor said a few years ago, "The gurus of America seem to think church growth is better than knowing God."[1] Bigger doesn't necessarily mean better. Not all large churches are healthy. A healthy church is one that brings glory to God through its godly attitudes.

Faith, Hope and Love

Paul identified three attitudes by which the Thessalonian church was glorifying God: "Your work of *faith*, labor of *love*, and steadfastness of *hope* . . ." (1 Thess. 1:3). John Calvin called the attributes of faith, hope and love "a brief description of true Christianity." You can't measure them, but they are shown in measurable ways. Faith, as James reminds us, produces the measurable quality of works. Love produces labor. Hope produces steadfastness.

Paul speaks of faith first because it is the prerequisite for salvation and sanctification—for all of the Christian life. It brings us back to the basics and establishes our priorities. We can get jazzed about the latest in technology or some new program or ministry concept coming down the pike, but what's important is still the same. The cross is still the cross. Sinners still need a Savior. The church still needs to fulfill her calling. Nothing really important has changed.

I think it's significant that Paul describes the salvation of the believers in Thessalonica in this way: "you turned to God from idols" (1 Thess. 1:9). Idolatry is more than worshipping images of animals. It's giving our allegiance to anything or anyone other than God. Paul, I believe, has a reason for the order of the words: they turned "to God from idols" and not "from idols to God." It's not that they were disgusted with their idolatry as much as they were in awe of the greatness of Christ. They heard the truth, and it set them free. It was like the old song says:

> *Turn your eyes upon Jesus,*
> *Look full in His wonderful face;*
> *And the things of earth will grow strangely dim*
> *In the light of His glory and grace.*[2]

When God begins to move in your midst, it becomes easier to turn from the idols of style, traditions, rules and regulations. Who needs all that when you have Jesus? Like the Thessalonians, our members got excited and turned to serve the living and true God. They began to offer willing service. Their worship was out of a pure heart, not out of duty to follow the program. We began to view life from an eternal perspective.

Not only did the Thessalonians work out their faith, but that led them to labor in their love. The word "labor" means work that results in weariness. It's hard work to love someone, and family members can be especially difficult to love because you don't get to pick them. As members of God's family, we don't get to pick those we love. We are to love everyone. To love someone is to want the best for them regardless of their merit or the cost to you. Too often we see crowds, but Jesus saw the people in the crowds. He always had time for the individual.

Thessalonica was full of con artists, religious hucksters, mystery religions with secret practices and false religions built on deceit. Paul said to them, "You haven't bought into that stuff. You've been delivered from it. You're the real deal, and I can see it in the way you labor in love."

In chapter three Paul writes, "May the Lord cause you to increase and abound in love [the source of ministry] for one another, and for all people [the scope of ministry], just as we also do for you; so that He may establish your hearts without blame in holiness [the standard for ministry] before our God and Father" (3:12–13). A loving church doesn't just ask, "How much does it cost?" A loving church asks, "What can we do to make a difference?" We have hundreds of members I call "second-mile saints." They are willing to go the second mile and have a "can do" attitude.

Twice a year we have two big events for the community. They are designed to help people in the city know who we are and what we are about. We want them to see the love of Christ as we serve them. The first event is a Halloween alternative called CandyFest. Hundreds of our members volunteer to build booths, staff the event, cook food and work security. In 2006 we had nearly 5,000 people attend. People from every walk of life showed up. We had thousands of parents with small children enjoying the safety of our campus and the spirit of our people. We have families in the church today who were first exposed to our ministry through CandyFest.

The second event is our Freedom Festival, a 4th of July celebration on our upper school campus. The event demands hundreds of hours of volunteer labor and hundreds of pounds of barbecue, ears of corn and watermelon. There are games, music, cakewalks and inflatables. We cap off the evening with a twenty-minute fireworks display that rivals our city's event. This has opened doors for us in the community like nothing else could. In 2006 we had over 6,000 people present on Sunday afternoon to celebrate our freedom as a nation.

Our goal is to labor in love for those in our community and for the glory of God. We want people to know we care. We want them to see how Christians are supposed to act.

We want people to know we care. We want them to see how Christians are supposed to act.

The last thing Paul mentions in First Thessalonians is their steadfastness of hope. They weren't chasing fads or programs. They were giving themselves to time-tested truths. This phrase indicates the stability of the church. They weren't busy trying to figure out who they were. They were grounded in grace, and hope empowered them to minister in the name of Jesus.

This is a tough world to minister in. With all the religious scandals trumpeted loudly in the media these days, we have to work harder to gain credibility. The world is watching, probing and examining us to see if we will walk our talk. Our attitude has to be "We're big enough to care, but not too big to do the little things." If we aren't willing to serve those across the street, what difference does it make if we make movies that are a success at the box office?

Regional Focus, Global Vision

God moved in my heart for a number of years about the kind of church we needed to be—not just a neighborhood church, but one that would impact our region. God was calling us to be good stewards of our gifts, finances, talents, facilities and resources. We adopted the motto "Touching the World from Albany, Georgia" to reflect this wider vision. I know what you're thinking: Where is Albany, Georgia? That's why the thought captured my attention.

In the 1960s Vance Havner was preaching in a local church that was complaining about all the things going on in the world. He said,

> It does little good for us to wring our hands and lament the inroads of television, ball games and other attractions on our church attendance. If we do not have enough vitality to compete with all this, maybe it doesn't matter much whether we have our meetings or not. If the gospel means so little to us that it can be sidetracked by every little side-show that blows into town, it wouldn't mean much if such people did gather to go through the motions of a dead faith. . . . We seem to be preaching and promoting something while most of its adherents wouldn't miss it much if they lost it![3]

The church too often makes excuses about why it can't do anything. We blame our location and sometimes even the Lord. I'm afraid we're guilty of complaining rather than seeking the Lord. We've also bought the lie that if God ever moves us to "that perfect church" or gives us "that perfect pastor," we'll be on our way to greatness. Too many leaders spend their lives looking over the fence at greener grass only to find out when they get there that it's artificial turf. They buy the lie, "If I were in that church, in that city and had that budget, I could do great things for God." But that's not where you are. God has placed you where you are for a reason. The Great Commission and the Great Commandment apply to us whether we are in the big city or the backwoods.

God has taught me that wherever I am, I need to be all there. I need to quit measuring myself by someone else, or being envious of another pastor or church, and just do what God has called me to do. Not everyone is supposed to do what we do. When people from other churches ask about our ministry, we do not try to get them to reproduce Sherwood. We encourage them to get alone with God and find out what He wants them to do.

Today we are no longer a neighborhood church. We have members who live in five counties and twenty-nine surrounding communities. We are a regional church. Some drive almost an hour one-way to come to church. Why? They've found a home here.

I believe one of the things that makes us unique is the way we do ministry. We are a pastor-led church. Our deacons serve and minister to widows. They are also responsible for keeping the unity of the church. We function with ministry teams like our finance team and personnel team. When we need another team, we form it—but we don't operate by committees. Someone has said the best committee is made up of three people, two of whom are dead. While others spend time debating, we are busy doing.

We also don't elect our deacons. They go through an interview and evaluation process with a team of five deacons.

We aren't interested in popular men, but godly leaders. Most of our deacons wouldn't win a popular election because they aren't looking for the spotlight. They are willing workers with a servant's heart. We present the deacons to the church for affirmation, not election.

We don't run the church by *Robert's Rules of Order* or a constitution and by-laws. No book or work of man is placed in authority over the Scriptures. We do everything decently and in order. Our business meetings are quarterly and last less than three minutes.

This church allows me to call the staff, lead the church and fill the pulpit. Some want a church where they have the power and preeminence. Sherwood is not that kind of church. We have a new members class to ensure that people understand what kind of church they are joining. We put it all out there for them beforehand so they can make an intelligent decision.

The question is not: "Is Sherwood right for me?" but "Am I right for Sherwood? Do I share their view of ministry and missions? Am I committed to the Scriptures as the sole authority? Do I want to be part of a Spirit-filled, Scripturally-sound congregation?" Some folks find out that they like us, but they don't want to be part of this kind of church. Sherwood is not for everyone, and we know that.

> *Many churches are watering down the gospel to get a crowd. You may end up with a crowd, but not a congregation.*

Not everyone wants to be part of a church where the Bible is considered inerrant, the miracles are believed as facts and Jesus is still the only way. Many churches are watering down the gospel to get a crowd. You may end up with a crowd, but not a congregation. Too many ministries seem to be shaky about what they believe. What we really need is to be *shaken* by what we believe.

We still need leaders like Joshua to call people to choose whom they will serve. We need men like Elijah who dare to confront the culture. We need men like Paul who aren't afraid to stand for truth over tradition. Some people don't want a church that rocks their world or their boat. It's the leader's job to raise the sails and catch the wind of the Spirit, even if it makes the fleshly a little seasick. It may be vogue to be vague, but it's not Biblical.

Not everyone wants to be part of a church where they can't be in charge or where people from all walks of life are welcomed. Today we have members from India, Africa, Asia, Pakistan, Chile, Argentina, Romania, the former Soviet Union and other parts of the world. We are a blended body of believers who look past the surface.

Many churches are dying because they wander in the wilderness and refuse to step out and believe God. God allowed us to have some wilderness-wandering years, but none of us who remained wanted to stay in that wilderness. We wanted to make a difference where we were. We want to train an army of followers of Jesus Christ to take the gospel to the world.

People often ask me how a church in Albany, Georgia, can do all that we do. We aren't a rich church. We're in a dying community. You probably can't get here from where you are because there are no interstates nearby. Factories and industries seem to be closing every year. My response is simple. As D.L. Moody said, "If God is your partner, make your plans big."[4] We have a big God. We believe Him for big things. We ask, seek and knock. We long for God to trust us with incredible opportunities that no one else seems to want.

We are able to do what we do because our church has a willing-worker mindset. They are faithful, available and teachable. Some of the ministries beyond the normal Sunday school and age-graded programs include:

- Feeding the homeless in the city every Thursday morning;

- Partnering with the Anchorage, a rehabilitation center for alcoholics and drug addicts;

- Partnering with other outreach and missions organizations in the community;

- Supporting Hospice here in Albany;

- The Sherwood Channel, a 24/7 television channel in partnership with FamNet and FAITH TV to provide religious programming to our community;

- "Home Connection," a thirty-minute televised Bible study designed to minister to the homebound and those in the hospital;

- "Walking in the Light," a thirty-minute televised program led by Pastor Daniel Simmons from Mt. Zion Baptist Church here in Albany;

- The Upward Sports program, which shares the love of Christ with parents and children (grades K-6th) through athletic programs (including basketball, soccer, flag football, and cheerleading) that build character and self-esteem;

- The Alpha Crisis Pregnancy Center where we counsel young ladies faced with a crisis pregnancy and possibly contemplating abortion;

- The Albany Biblical Counseling Center where we offer Biblically-based counseling for a small fee.

The majority of these ministries are run by volunteers. We might have a staff member in charge of the ministry, but hundreds of people fill the gaps to make these ministries happen.

One thing I know is this: When people are hard at work serving Jesus, they don't have time to be critical, caustic or casual about their faith. When your hands are to the plow, you aren't worried about anything but getting your task done. I thank God every day for the people of Sherwood who have put their hands to the plow. They've stayed in the field when it would have been easier to bail out and go somewhere else. Their lives are hidden with Christ in God. Their service is the outgrowth of the indwelling Holy Spirit.

Dinner on the grounds of the sports park property

7

Relationships Are Essential

*O*NE DAY while serving in a previous church the chairman of the pulpit committee came into my office. "Michael," he said, "there are sixteen people in this church that hate your guts."

I was shocked! "How do you know? Who are they?"

"I don't know who they all are," he replied, "but you don't need to know their names. They were here with the pastor before you and the one before that and the one before that. They hated all those who came before you, and they will hate the man who follows you. *They've always been here, and they'll always be here.*"

"Do you think I can outlive them?"

He had a smirk on his face as he responded, "No! When they die, their spirit falls on someone else. There will never be fifteen or eighteen. The number will always be sixteen. If you can live with that fact and not focus on it, you'll be able to survive."

In his own unique, tongue-in-cheek way, that pulpit committee chairman taught me an important truth. I think it was John Maxwell who said the average pastor leaves a church because of eight people. Of course eight can feel like eight hundred. All of us are one bow to pride away from someone setting out to undermine the work God has called us to do. That's why healthy relationships are so important.

In fact, they're essential to revival. Why? Because revival involves change, and change is a funny thing. We all hate it, but at the same time, we all need it. Healthy change can only occur in the context of healthy relationships. To make change—whether it's change in the church or change for a dollar bill—you need to have change in your pocket. It takes time to build up "change in your pocket," which comes through consistency, admitting your need for others and learning from your mistakes—these are the keys to healthy relationships.

> *Healthy change can only occur in the context of healthy relationships.*

Pastor/Church Relationships

The principle of taking time to develop relationships is especially crucial between the pastor and his flock. Just because people call you "Pastor" doesn't automatically mean you *are* the pastor. That takes time. It takes time for sheep to learn the voice of the shepherd and to know the difference between a hireling and a true shepherd. Too often a pastor makes the mistake of walking into a new field of service and upsetting the sheep by trying to make wholesale changes.

Someone has said that turning a church around is like trying to turn an oil tanker around in the ocean. If you turn it too quickly, it will tip over. The shift will be too much, too soon. If you turn it slowly, the ship can make the turn successfully.

Ironically, according to some studies, the average tenure of a pastor in America is two to three years. Don't even think about making a lot of changes if you aren't planning to be there for the long haul. You can't shepherd a church if you only see it as a stepping stone to another church! Serving the Body demands an investment.

I realize even in saying this that I was only in my first pastorate three years. In reality, I wasn't looking to leave. In fact, I had turned down several opportunities to move on. We loved our house, the town and the staff. We were beginning to see a movement of the Holy Spirit among God's people that encouraged us. If God had not made it abundantly clear that my time there was over, I would not have left.

It's easy to quit. It's easy to send out a résumé and look for greener pastures. It's much harder to stand and take the heat. If the Lord Himself couldn't please everyone, what makes us think we can? You have to find the remnant, the prayer warriors, those longing for more than Sunday-morning religion and build relationships with them.

I believe most pastors leave just when God is ready to break through. I called Ron Dunn one day complaining about some things that were happening. He said, "Michael, stop it. You are making me miss the pastorate." I got the point. The pastorate is a lonely, tough job. Deal with it. Nobody promised a rose garden. You need people you can be honest with and who can be honest with you. You need to be willing for them to give you a subtle (or not so subtle) rebuke when needed.

Early in our ministry at Sherwood, we established groups of men to meet with the staff for prayer. For over fifteen years I've met one morning a week with a group of men to pray together and seek godly counsel from them. They have listened to me blow off steam. They have encouraged me, cautioned me and prayed for me when I wasn't very lovable. They've seen me at my best and in my flesh.

Through the years the group has changed in size, but three men have stayed with me through it all. John Dees, Ron Dorminey and Roy Pippin have been faithful to meet me, buy me breakfast and see how I'm doing. I'm not sure I would have survived a few tough times if it had not been for their prayers and support.

John and Ron still meet with me faithfully, but Roy is no longer able due to health reasons. I remember Roy telling me one day, when he was serving as deacon chairman, that he was willing to give his life to see revival in our church. I'm still haunted by that statement as I've watched his health deteriorate through these last few years. If I could ask God to give every pastor one thing, it wouldn't be a larger salary or more perks; it would be three praying men who would stand in the trenches with them.

Staff Relationships

Staff relationships are obviously a key component in a multi-staff church. You can't just fill slots and look for the cheapest help possible. You have to find people who fit the puzzle. It takes the Lord to bring together a team that is willing to lay aside their personal agendas and follow the vision of a leader.

The late T.W. Wilson was Billy Graham's right-hand man for decades. T.W. was a leader in his own right—a successful evangelist, pastor and preacher—but because of his belief in what God was doing through Billy's life, he laid aside his plans and his agenda to serve Dr. Graham.

I wonder if there will ever be another evangelist like Billy because it would be hard to find another team like the one he had. Think about Cliff Barrows, Bev Shea, Grady Wilson, George Wilson, T.W. Wilson and a host of others who were great leaders in their own right. They chose to decrease so the ministry could prosper. They were willing to be servants. They didn't want to be celebrities. They didn't use their position as a stepping- stone to their own platform. They were willing to stand in the shadows because they were sensitive enough to the Spirit to see what God was doing through their friend Billy Graham.

Every leader should pray for a team that will go to the wall with him. Loyalty, integrity and longevity are endangered species in the ministry. Character is often lacking.

> *You can't grow a great church on someone's ego.*

Too many are asking, "What's in it for me? How can you help me get ahead?" You can't grow a great church on someone's ego.

Today I believe we have the healthiest staff we've had in our history. I'm watching their kids grow up before my eyes. I'm watching some people who were green when they came here develop into seasoned players. We laugh together, pray together and support and encourage one another.

I've been blessed with two incredible men who have served as executive pastor—John Hemken and Jim McBride. The executive pastor runs the day-to-day affairs so I can set myself aside for prayer and the preaching of the Word. John, our first executive pastor, had been a successful businessman with Proctor and Gamble. He was serving as a deacon when I asked him to join our staff.

John was a nuts-and-bolts, no-frills kind of guy. He stood in the gap for me more than once, for which I'll be eternally grateful. Our relationship was blessed by a mutual respect. He understood what it meant to serve the pastor, carry out the vision and move the organization forward.

During John's tenure we built almost 100,000 square feet of new space—a worship center, new choir suite and media center. Because he kept the pencil to the paper, we went from being three months behind and $500,000 over budget to finishing six weeks early and coming in under budget. I never worried about the project because I knew that John would handle it.

John was the one who started our emphasis on staff prayer groups, meeting at 6 a.m. once a week. He led the finance team in prayer every Tuesday at 7 a.m. John led our intercessory prayer ministry and had a real passion for it. He helped me get the first groups praying during the worship service.

Jim McBride, who followed John as executive pastor, had been a plant manager for Coca-Cola. Like John, he was a respected businessman in the community and recognized as a leader by other laity in the church. He too was serving as a deacon when he came on staff.

Jim's initial responsibility was chairing the committee overseeing Sherwood Christian Academy. He came at a time of conflict, and while some might have shied away from such a difficult situation, Jim took the position and began to manage the chaos.

Soon after, we asked Jim to serve as pastor of the school. The headmaster and faculty understood that in this position he was responsible for the spiritual leadership of the school. In addition, he approved all decisions regarding hiring and employment. He had his hands full.

Jim proved to be the right man at the right time. The school went through a pruning process, and some left because they disagreed with the way the school was run. It wasn't easy, and we probably wouldn't have the school we have today if Jim had not walked away from a successful business career to tackle this ministry.

He often worked closely with John and me, helping us with ministry decisions and other pressing issues. It was natural for him to step into the role of executive pastor when John left. His background in the Marines has served him well; he's a soldier at heart with a love for people. He is a godly father and husband and one of the most disciplined readers I know. I don't know of a man in our church that doesn't respect him.

I sometimes sit in awe of how calm Jim can be in the midst of a storm. At times when I've wanted to blow up, he has calmly let me vent and then has given me other options. Ninety-nine percent of the time he's right. His day-to-day management allows me to spend more time with the staff developing personal relationships and helping them catch a vision for the church.

John and Jim have been to me what T.W. Wilson and others were to Billy Graham. Whatever success or recognition I might ever have, I owe it to these two men standing with me, by me and for me through good and bad. If you want to see God rain down revival, surround yourself with great men—men you can love, trust, bare your heart to and be real

> *If you want to see God rain down revival, surround yourself with great men—men you can love, trust, bare your heart to and be real with.*

with. My hope and prayer is that one day when it's time for us to pass the baton, Jim and I will ride off into the sunset together.

Multicultural Relationships

I grew up at a time when schools were being integrated, and there was much strife related to the civil rights movement. When I was a student at Mississippi College in the early '70s, I served as a part-time youth minister at a church in the Jackson area. We started a youth visitation program, and on our first night out, a group of students led a family of five African-American youth to Christ. The students came back to the church encouraged and excited, but the deacons went into an uproar.

Unbeknownst to me, the church had a policy not to allow blacks into membership. During this same time I was writing a weekly student ministry column. One week I ended my article with a quote from Dr. Martin Luther King. I was fired within five days. I count it as a badge of honor that a church so full of hatred and prejudice would fire me. I would certainly never want to serve a church that was so narrow-minded.

It grieves me that in the 21st century we still have many of our churches divided along racial lines. Some are stuck in the mid-20th century when it comes to race relations. This is not just a southern problem. I've seen it everywhere I've served. Whether it's African-American, Caucasian, Hispanic, Asian or Native American, people can't seem to understand that in Christ there is no divide.

Eric and Ramona Reese are members of our church. They are some of the only African-American missionaries sent out by the International Mission Board of the Southern Baptist Convention. Eric and Ramona have a wonderful ministry in Brazil. While home on furlough, Eric went to a Southern Baptist church in another state to share what God was doing through the gifts of His people. The church held Eric back-stage until it was time for him to speak. When he walked into the room, fifty people stood up and left. When Eric finished speaking, the head of the church missions organization said to him, "Young man, I think what you said is nice, and I appreciate your sincerity. But we all know there aren't going to be any blacks in heaven."

How can we ask God for revival while entertaining those kinds of thoughts? How can we reach the world with the gospel and say we're committed to the Great Commission if we think that "whosoever will" only means "people like me"? Vance Havner wrote, "Our greatest hindrance in the church today is within our own ranks. We can't get to the goal for stumbling over our own team. We furnish our greatest interference."[1]

By the grace of God I have found a beloved brother and a kindred spirit in an African-American pastor, Dr. Daniel Simmons. He and I have worked to partner our churches for the last ten years. While some folks are consumed with building barriers, and others want to pretend issues don't exist, we are committed to building bridges.

God has blessed our efforts. We now call each other "co-pastor," and the members of our two churches share one spirit. His people call me "co-pastor" when I see them in the community. My members call him "co-pastor" as well. He is the one true pastor friend I have in this community. Together we are tackling the giants that seek to divide our community.

One of my great joys here has been the relationship with Daniel and his church, Mt. Zion Baptist. In Albany, the thought of a predominantly white church and a predominantly African-American church forming a partnership is not the norm. There are a few churches that give a token nod on "Race Relations Sunday," but for the most part they aren't interested in really getting to know their brothers in Christ.

Changing a mindset doesn't happen overnight. You have to deal with it Biblically and consistently.

Changing a mindset doesn't happen overnight. You have to deal with it Biblically and consistently. If you're in a situation where people refuse to reach out and cross socioeconomic or racial barriers, you can't make that change by snapping your fingers. You must take the time and effort to express compassion, love people and teach them to love others. America is becoming such a diverse culture that this is no longer an option for any of us; we've got to learn how to relate to one another.

My friendship with Daniel started in 1994 when a flood devastated Albany. Mt. Zion suffered extensive damage when the Flint River overflowed its banks. As soon as he could get there, our executive pastor took them a check for several thousand dollars to help them in the crisis. Throughout the following years, Daniel and I built a relationship.

I've now had the honor of preaching on his anniversary and at several events in his church. Together we have hosted events featuring our adult choirs, Tony Evans, TRUTH and Warren Wiersbe. We worked together with Warren Wiersbe for two years on a conference called "Bridge Builders," which brought African-American and white pastors together to be trained and encouraged in their work. Every year Daniel preaches at our ReFRESH Conference and always brings a powerful message from the Word. He is one of the most gifted preachers I know.

The Georgia State Legislature has even recognized us for our work in racial reconciliation in Albany. In January 2003 we were given the first ever Unity Award at the Martin Luther King Celebration in Albany for our efforts to build bridges.

Put to the Test

The greatest test of our relationship was during an area-wide crusade planned for our city. A successful businessman was supporting the event financially and planned to bring in a nationally known evangelist. He had already gone to several African-American pastors, and they were willing to participate. We signed on as well, believing it would be something God could use.

Unfortunately it didn't take long for the idea to be shot down by several predominately white churches that evidently didn't want African-Americans telling them how to do a crusade. It seemed like a flashback to the 1950s.

About five years later the same group that had shot down the crusade announced they were planning an event with the same organization. They didn't bother to contact one African-American pastor. They planned it, set the date, announced the preacher and then asked everyone to get on board. One African-American pastor put it this way: "They asked us to get on the parade float after it had already been designed and built. We wanted the courtesy of having input into the design of the float."

This was another defining moment for me, for Sherwood and for this community. I knew in my heart that I couldn't support these men after the way they had treated the black churches, and I told them so.

Sherwood was immediately tagged as being uncooperative. They were saying we didn't care if sinners went to hell. Letters were written to the editor. Still, I didn't want to participate in treating someone as a second-class citizen or a second-class church.

As the crusade approached, the heat was on. One of the leaders came to my office to ask what could be done to get the black churches on board. I told him he had to repent, ask their forgiveness and then see if anything changed. But it was too little, too insincere and too late.

The crusade did not reach the crowds they anticipated. A picture in the local paper with entire sections empty was sent to me with the empty seats circled and a caption that read: "Sherwood's and Mt. Zion's section." I now understand a little of what it means to be blacklisted. We sided with what I believe was right and moral, and I still feel we did the right thing. I would do it again, and I believe Daniel would too.

> *We sided with what I believe was right and moral, and I still feel we did the right thing.*

If it had not been for the relationships I had built in our church and with Mt. Zion, these decisions could have easily gone south in a hurry. Instead God has blessed both of our churches since that moment. People discovered we were serious about being partners, and since then I've been asked to preach in several African-American churches in our area.

I've asked Daniel to share some of his insights about our relationship. We labor in a tough field. Our churches are different, yet in many ways the same, but this relationship has been one of the most enriching, encouraging and edifying of my entire life.

Daniel Simmons:

Our relationship with Michael and Sherwood Baptist Church began in 1994 after the flood hit Albany. All the local churches worked together across racial and denominational lines. I met John Hemken, Sherwood's executive pastor, who introduced me to Michael, and our friendship began.

Unfortunately, most of the relationships formed during the flood dissolved once the initial working stages were over. Most churches went back to their respective corners, but Michael continued moving forward with our friendship. The thing that really joined our hearts was the turmoil we experienced during an area-wide crusade. Michael and I stood together and took the brunt of criticism and misunderstanding. From that point on, Sherwood and Mt. Zion continued to link arms.

The Bible says that one man sharpens another as iron sharpens iron. I've learned a lot from Michael, and he's learned a few things from me. I believe if you're going somewhere, you can learn from somebody who's already at the place you're headed. Michael has helped me greatly in the areas of membership, organizational structure and budgeting. For example, when our budget passed the one million mark, I knew his budget was way past that, so I talked to him. Michael taught me to prepare in advance for what you expect God to do. So instead of managing a million-dollar budget, I started managing a two-million-dollar budget while waiting on God to provide.

Michael is well-read and often shares with me the best books he's read. I have a passion to help other ministers, and Michael shares that same passion, so it has been a real blessing to do that through the Bridge Builders Conference and the ReFRESH Conference.

I think our partnership is a living testimony that people who are Christ-centered can overcome any worldly barrier. Race is a worldly barrier. Denomination is a worldly barrier. One of the things our city has to admit is that many of our leaders in the church and in the community have not been truthful. We hear all the time that the races in Albany cannot come together and will not work together. We've proven that blacks and whites can come together and trust each other. I trust Michael, and I feel that he trusts me. Our people trust each other. We've shown the leaders in this town that they're just making excuses.

For the two churches, the partnership has expanded our thinking of what God wants His church to look like. There are things Sherwood and Mt. Zion do differently, so we're always learning from each other. My congregation feels good about the relationship. I know the Sherwood members do because I meet them all over town. They stop me and call me "co-pastor." My people do the same with Michael. The partnership has been a tremendous help to both our ministries.

We have faced some opposition. Initially it came from a couple of people within the church who were suspicious. Given the history of Albany and the two churches, why would Sherwood want to associate with us? They advised me to move with caution because they thought something was up. Some told me not to move forward with the relationship, but we did anyway.

Outside, primarily within the church community, some peers and friends have been very critical of our relationship. People tend to demonize you when they can't find anything legitimate to criticize you about. So I've been demonized for crossing racial lines and having fellowship with Sherwood. I've been called everything from "the white man's boy" to "a sell-out." My peers have asked, "If you want to fellowship with somebody, why don't you fellowship with us? Are we too little for you? You've got to go over there with the big church."

But, because of this relationship, people in the community have paid attention. Sometimes the newspaper or television stations would call me for an interview. Michael and I have occasionally done those interviews together, and I've also been criticized for that.

In spite of some oppostion, God has blessed our partnership. We have learned from the ministries of Sherwood and have made our ministries better. We've developed some ministries as a direct result of conversations I've had with Michael. Because of Sherwood's TV ministry, I've had the opportunity to broadcast a weekly Bible study. People are coming from all the surrounding counties simply because they heard about us on television. People have joined Mt. Zion and have said to me, "I saw what you were doing with Sherwood, and I think that's what the church ought to be. I want to be part of a progressive church like that."

I've gotten to meet John Maxwell, Warren Wiersbe and other men—opportunities I probably would not have had otherwise. I take what I've learned from these men and use it at church, and the ministry expands. The ReFRESH Conference has been a blessing and has introduced me to men like Ken Jenkins and Bill Stafford. I've introduced Michael to other African-American pastors, and they've gotten to know and love him.

We recently put up a sign on our new property that says, "Expanding Our Facility to Expand Our Capacity to Reach the World for Christ." We believe it is going to do just that.

We've purchased 109 acres and plan to do something similar to what Sherwood is doing, with a sports complex and a fitness center. The possibilities are unending. My desire, however, is not to duplicate or become the next Sherwood. We want to learn from Sherwood's best, mold it to fit Mt. Zion and move ahead.

We are "preparing for rain."

Daniel Simmons preaching at Sherwood

Michael Catt preaching at Mt. Zion Baptist Church

8

Plow the Field God Gives You

*T*HE STORY in the movie *Facing the Giants* about two farmers who prayed for rain continues to haunt me. It is a parable for our day.

I am convinced that every generation is given an opportunity to plow a field for God. If they fail they are relegated to wilderness wanderings. Like the children of Israel, some of God's people don't want to pay the price to take the land. They would rather eat dust and bury the dead than see a harvest and bring those dead in sin to saving faith.

If you study churches, you know that often a church will be great in one generation and falter in the next. Rarely will you find a church that had the largest Sunday school in the 1970s even mentioned today. Either they sat on their blessings and got comfortable, or they refused to keep going and growing. For whatever reason, it seems as if the cloud of blessing and opportunity has passed them by, at least for a season.

There are windows of opportunity before us that are unparalleled in the history of the church. Not since the invention of the printing press or the development of mass transportation have we had so many opportunities to spread the gospel and touch the world. With resources come responsibilities. We must seize opportunities when they arise. Hesitation can

_____ ≈ _____

We must seize opportunities when they arise. Hesitation can be fatal to our future.

_____

be fatal to our future. If a church fails to act in the right moment because of unbelief or unwillingness to step out in faith, the fellowship may wander in the wilderness for decades.

This came home to me in the early 1980s while riding with my pastor when serving a church in the Atlanta area. He took me to the intersection of Interstate 285 and Interstate 75 and told me how he had envisioned relocating the church to that plot of land. Acre after acre of land had been available at a very reasonable price.

"With the projected growth of our area I realized the growth of our church would necessitate further development of our facilities," my pastor said. "I took five of the most influential men in our church to a lovely hillside overlooking a two-lane road. From that vantage point I told them some day a major interchange would corner on the property that would carry over 200,000 cars a day. We could relocate and reach an inestimable clientele. They demurred, saying the property would cost $10,000 an acre and was too expensive."

Today twelve lanes of traffic cross at that intersection,

and the property is valued at more than $250,000 per acre. A deteriorating community now surrounds the original church plant.

A book that impacted me greatly in my early days of ministry was Nelson Price's *I've Got to Play on Their Court*. The book is based on the philosophy of Roswell Street Baptist Church where Dr. Price served as pastor for many years. I've often called the book the *Purpose Driven Church* of the 1970s, as Dr. Price was used by God to build a mega-church before anyone knew what a mega-church was.

Dr. Price was one of the most innovative and aggressive pastors I've ever known. He had a passion for young people. He originated events like Student Appreciation Night where thousands of high school students would gather for a rally at the church. Having organized four of those events, I can tell you it was one of the most electrifying ministries I've ever been a part of.

Dr. Price was always trying to determine the best way to impact the culture. He wrote a daily column for the local paper. He was probably one of the best known personalities in the Atlanta area. Under his leadership a sleepy little Southern Baptist church became a powerful witness for Christ. When I asked Dr. Price to tell me more about his ideas behind the book, he sent me the following email:

> Paige Patterson describes *I've Got to Play on Their Court* as the first book written by a pastor on church growth. As a high school freshman, I naively asked our basketball coach why we didn't play all of our games on our home court. His short answer shaped my philosophy of ministry: "If we want them to play on our court we have to play on their court."
> I began identifying popular places and events in the

broader community and started relating to those involved there. By identifying with them and their concerns, I was able to engage their interest. One "court" on which I played was the court of community leaders. I resolved to become a first-name friend with every elected official, school principal and leader of any kind in the community.

The philosophy was to reach the total community and not just the local congregation. I clipped news articles and mailed them with a note to persons in the news every week. One such note resulted in the salvation of four members of one family. One of those youths grew up to become the sound manager for all the Billy Graham crusades.

After having been in the community for one year, I baked a cake and took it to the editor of the local newspaper on the anniversary of the founding of the paper. He responded by asking me to write a weekly column for the paper. That column is the most read weekly column and has been running for forty-one years. It is now in seventeen newspapers.

I observed the obvious competitive spirit of students regarding their schools. I came up with the wild and crazy idea of using this competitive spirit to attract them to church. It took a very understanding and forgiving congregation to support the idea.

Clubs, teams and individual students from each high school were invited to the church. We encouraged them to wear their school colors, provide athletic uniforms and pennants to display and bring their cheerleading squads. We awarded trophies to the schools for the largest number in attendance, the highest percentage of students present, the most colorful group and the most spirited group. It struck a cord and became an annual event. A prominent athlete spoke, and the music was the kind appreciated by youth. We also made an appeal for students to make a life commitment to Christ. Many adult community leaders of today were won to Christ in those rowdy rallies. Thank the Lord for an understanding congregation. It was not "doing church as usual."

When considering a concept, I kept it in the "prayer incubator" for a period of time. Not wanting to share an immature idea before its time, I occasionally asked the congregation to pray for a matter in the "prayer incubator." Many of those ideas hatched. One was our television ministry, "Come Alive."

For five years I prayed for the opportunity to reach metro Atlanta through television. A call came from a television station with an opening for our program during the week that we concluded a campaign which raised more money for a building program than any other church in our denomination. Having appealed to the congregation to give sacrificially to the building program, I was now faced with going back and asking for more money or with missing out on the opportunity altogether.

The following Sunday I explained the recent development to the congregation and expressed appreciation for their sacrificial commitments. I then explained that if there were enough people who would commit one more dollar per week, we would launch the television ministry. Uncomplainingly and unselfishly they did. Their giving ultimately resulted in a television ministry that reached all fifty states, five nations and the islands of the Caribbean. It was the largest and last of the live worship services broadcast on a network station in America.

Throughout my time at Roswell Street, God honored the prayers and responses of the people. The title of a recording that Jerry Clower made at the church says it all: "Ain't God Good!"

The reason I share this with you is that we can't just invite people to come to church; we have to go where they are. We have to engage the culture. We have to meet people at the point of their need. Isn't that what Jesus did? He engaged people on the dusty roads and in the villages. He didn't invite people to the synagogue. He walked the streets. God in flesh touched humanity where they lived.

What do you weep about? What breaks your heart? Where is your burden?

What do you weep about? What breaks your heart? Where is your burden? Do you recall Psalm 137 when the children of Israel were weeping as they "remembered Zion"? Zion represented everything good about God and His blessings. They were in captivity because of their disobedience. Sin had poisoned their potential, and they had wasted their window of opportunity.

What drives you and motivates you? What has captivated your heart? Where's the passion in your ministry and church? If we are going to make an impact on this culture, we can't sit in our comfortable pews and daydream. We have to put our hands to the plow and get to work. We will never make an impact in a comfort zone.

Thomas Edison said, "Show me a thoroughly satisfied man, and I will show you a failure." Sir Francis Drake expressed much the same thing in a little prayer that I've been drawn to again while writing this book:

Disturb us, O Lord,
 when we are too well-pleased with ourselves;
 when our dreams have come true because we have
  dreamed too little,
 when we arrived safely because we sailed too close to
  the shore.
Disturb us, O Lord,
 when with the abundance of things we possess,
  we have lost our thirst for the Waters of Life,
 having fallen in love with life, we have ceased to
  dream of eternity.
 And in our efforts to build a new earth,
  we have allowed our vision of the new heaven to dim.
Disturb us, O Lord,
 to dare more boldly, to venture on wider seas,
  where storms will show Your mastery;
 where losing sight of land, we shall find the stars.
We ask You to push back the horizon of our hopes,
  and to push us into the future with strength,
   courage, hope and love.

Hosea said to Israel, "Break up your fallow ground, for it is time to seek the LORD" (10:12). Fallow ground is unproductive and undisturbed. It has to be broken up, tilled and prepared for the seed. The rocks and weeds have to be removed. The tilling has to be deep for there to be a bountiful harvest.

What if the disciples had just sat around and played "Remember when?" games after the ascension? What if the church in Acts had rested on its laurels after the day of Pentecost? What if they had refused to embrace Gentiles? When I read the story of the early church, I realize they were passionately committed to meeting spiritual, physical and emotional needs. They taught the Word, and they also lived it out.

What if William Carey had listened to his critics and not gone to the mission field? What if Martin Luther had kept his thoughts to himself? These men took advantage of the opportunities set before them and changed the world around them. They plowed the ground and got to work. D. L. Moody said, "I am only one, but I am one. I cannot do everything, but I can do something. And that which I can do, by the grace of God, I will do."[1]

God is looking for one man, one church, one person who will dare to be different—one who will take Him at His word. One who will see the fields white unto harvest and will pay the price to make an eternal impact.

God has given Sherwood a field far larger than our founding fathers imagined. When this church was established in 1955, it was in a new neighborhood on the growing edge of town accessible by dirt roads. Today that spot is surrounded by neighborhoods and businesses. We started with six acres. Today we have over one hundred acres of property.

After acquiring property on Old Pretoria Road and expanding our upper school campus to that location, we still had dreams of a sports and recreation park for outreach and Upward Sports ministries. The church owned some mission property, but water and sewage problems made it less appealing for us to build there. In March 2001, Jim McBride stopped by Ray Abbot's convenience store adjacent to the upper campus. Jim and Ray discussed the property surrounding the campus as they walked through a tract of land owned by Byron Henderson and another parcel owned by Bubba Pippin.

After we discussed his findings, Jim contacted Mr. Henderson and Mr. Pippin, and both agreed to sell us their land. While we were working through this process, our mission property sold, enabling us to purchase the properties adjacent to the school in November 2001. We gained an additional fourteen acres of land and still had money left over to begin clearing for the sports complex.

We have a saying around Sherwood: Whoever wants the next generation the most will get them. In a culture where everyone and everything is vying for the attention and affections of our youth, the church must fight for the hearts and lives of our kids. One of the major influences in the lives of children and families is sports and recreation. In his book, *Sports Ministry for Churches*, Tommy Yessick writes:

> *Whoever wants the next generation the most will get them.*

> More than 75 percent of people in America either participate in, watch or read about a sporting event of some type every single day. It is not even unusual for sports stories to bump other national issues from the headlines. While not everyone is interested in sports, a lot are, either directly or indirectly. Are we, as ministers, missing a golden opportunity to involve hundreds in a ministry that seeks to build the Kingdom and nurture Christian development?[2]

For the past two and a half years, Sherwood has used the Upward Sports programs as a bridge between the church and the community. During that time we've had over 1,500 participants, and sixty-nine people have prayed to receive Christ. Because of the impact of this ministry and the importance of sports in the lives of so many families, we are building a sports complex for future generations. The complex will house baseball, t-ball and softball fields; a fishing pond; a walking track; soccer fields; tennis and volleyball courts; horse stables; an open-air pavilion and much more.

Tour of new sports park property

John 4:35 says, "Behold, I say to you, lift up your eyes and look at the fields, for they are already white for harvest." The ministry of sports and recreation at Sherwood is driven by this mandate. The fields are white here in South Georgia, and if we go and do the work of showing Jesus to Albany through sports, we will see a harvest. That is what drives us.

Recently a young couple transferred to Albany from Ohio. Albany was not in their original plans, but God had a specific purpose for them here. The couple began visiting Sherwood, and after a few months the husband began playing basketball at our Recreation Outreach Center with some of the guys in his Sunday school class. Before each game someone shares a passage of Scripture and a short devotional. This young man heard the gospel one evening and began to ask questions after the game. In the middle of the basketball court, he prayed to receive Christ that night.

He and his wife are being transferred back to Ohio after their short stay with us, but they are confident that the Lord had them here for a purpose.

Stuart Briscoe said, "The average Christian is like an old iron bed; firm on both ends but sagging in the middle."[3] Many believers know they are saved and know they are going to heaven, but they are apathetic about what's happening in between. My friend Mark Harris, a former member of 4Him, wrote a song entitled "The Line Between the Two." It's about what happens during that dash we put on our tombstones between the date of birth and the date of death. That dash represents our lives. Is it significant? Will you make a difference with the life God gives you?

There are three people sitting where you are right now. One is the person you are at this very moment. Another is the person you could become if you choose to live your life in the flesh and fail to press ahead. A third is the person you could be for God if you put your hands to the plow and never look back. But I don't see many people or churches

I don't see many people or churches storming the gates of hell. Too many are holding the fort, hoping Jesus will come back before they cave in.

storming the gates of hell. Too many are holding the fort, hoping Jesus will come back before they cave in.

When Jesus came to live in us, He did not come to be a passive nonentity; He came to be an active reality. Christ in you is your hope of glory. You have been crucified with Christ, and He is now your life. Ron Dunn writes, "It is foolish to ask God to give you more blessings when you haven't lived out the blessings you already have."[4] Let's admit it. We all know more than we're living up to!

Our calling is beyond the four walls of Sherwood Baptist Church, and your calling must go beyond your four walls. In Acts 5:16 we read that "the people from the cities in the vicinity of Jerusalem were coming together." A church can have an impact beyond its boundaries. The gospel is just too great to put a lid on it!

A survey taken in the 1990s said that out of one hundred people, twenty-three don't have a clue what they want; sixty-seven know what they want but don't know how to get it; ten know what they want and how to get it; and eight of those ten are unwilling to pay the price. So only two out of one hundred reach their goals. I would say those numbers are true of the church. Out of every one hundred churches, you might find two that are stretching, sacrificing and serving to their potential.

Steve Brown says the difference between a donkey and a thoroughbred is how they respond when they feel threatened. Thoroughbreds will stand in a circle and face each other, then kick out their hind legs. Donkeys will stand facing the enemy with their backs to each other and kick each other. We need more thoroughbred churches who will storm the gates of hell and not kick each other in the process. We cannot settle for less than God's best.

Upward soccer game at sports park

9

Growing Pains and Moviemaking

*A*S THE MEMBERS of Sherwood embraced the vision "to touch the world from Albany, Georgia," we sensed our need for expansion. We were bursting at the seams in three morning services in our previous worship center. We moved forward with a building program called "Future Generations" to provide a new worship center, music offices, choir and orchestra suites, a bookstore and a chapel.

Prior to moving into our new facility, we embraced a "prepare for rain" philosophy. We held an Easter service there in 2000—almost a year before the building was completed. All we had was a concrete floor and a roof over our heads. We worked quickly to move air conditioning ducts out of the way and prepare the floor for 2,800 chairs. Evangelist Jay Strack spoke that Easter morning, and thirty-nine people gave their lives to Christ. We didn't have all the amenities of a finished space, but God blew through that Easter service in power.

As we progressed with the building, we began to mark it for God. We bought hundreds of permanent markers so members could write on the floor before we laid carpet and tile. The senior adults wrote Scriptures and prayers on the floor of the chapel. The choir and orchestra wrote Bible verses, music and prayers on the floor of the choir room. I remember praying with Terri, Mark and Katy Willard (our minister of music and his wife), John and Kathleen Hemken and Alex Kendrick that night after everyone had left. The glory of God filled the choir room that evening.

One Sunday afternoon I invited the deacons, staff and Sunday school teachers to join me in the worship center to write verses on the platform. All along the walls and the floor of the platform are hundreds of prayers, verses and quotes. I marked off a six-foot section near the pulpit area to write statements that impacted my life and verses about preaching the Word. On the spot where the pulpit now stands I wrote the words of Charles Spurgeon: "Let him who stands here and does not preach Jesus be accursed." The quote is a reminder of Sherwood's serious commitment to be a people of the Book.

As we prepared to move into the new facility, we encountered many obstacles.

As we prepared to move into the new facility, we encountered many obstacles. We didn't pass a few inspections, and there was a failure in the alarm system. The entire computerized alarm system had to be replaced in twenty-four hours in order for us to get a certificate of occupancy. God had it all under control, but we often sweated through it.

In February 2001 on the last night in our old worship center, we partook of the Lord's Supper together. Less than twenty people knew what I had up my sleeve to honor the Lord and those who were faithful on Sunday nights. I've been in enough building programs to know that some folks show up for the big event and think that's their ticket into heaven. I wanted to give the Sunday night crowd a little something special.

After the Lord's Supper service, I asked people to get up and join me in the new worship center for the remainder of the evening. We were going to celebrate and worship in the new facilities a week before our official opening. (As I often tell people, if you miss Sunday nights at Sherwood, you miss the best part!)

We gathered in the atrium and read Scripture, then walked in together. With the choir leading us we all sang "Let Your Glory Fall," and we sensed God's power descend. It was evident to many of us that God was going to use these facilities as an outpost, a city of refuge and a center for revival by His grace. We still live with a spirit of anticipation and expectation.

In the book *The Three Success Secrets of Shamgar,* Jay Strack shares the story behind a statue by the Greek sculptor, Lysippus, who lived four centuries before Christ:

> My favorite work of Lysippus is his male statue of Opportunity. With careful detail, Lysippus carved a powerfully symbolic image of Opportunity. It is the image of a power-

fully built man with wings on his feet and a huge lock of hair on his forehead. Seen from the back, however, the man's head is bald. What do these symbols mean?

The winged feet mean that Opportunity is moving swiftly and won't be here long. The lock of hair on Opportunity's forehead is something to grab onto and hold, to keep Opportunity from slipping away. But the baldness of the back of Opportunity's head tells us that, once it has passed you by, there is nothing you can take hold of. If you let Opportunity go, it may never be within your reach again.[1]

The move into our new facilities was a crucial step in seizing opportunities that God sends our way. They provide us with more space to accommodate people, thus expanding our influence and our effectiveness in ministry. We had prepared our fields for rain, and we were now ready for God to send the showers . . . and He has! During recent years we have seen God move in our midst in unbelievable ways. One of those was the launching of Sherwood Pictures and our first film.

The Making of a Movie

When the vision was cast for shooting our first movie, *Flywheel,* some members were skeptical, but most were excited. They were ready to believe God for another amazing and unique opportunity to touch the world from Albany, Georgia. Sherwood had been molded into a swift, seaworthy sailing vessel, and ships aren't made for port, but for sailing. We spent many years sailing before the idea of making movies ever surfaced. The congregation had been taught how to dream big dreams, think outside the box and believe

God for the impossible . . . and we had seen God come through time and time again.

I met Alex Kendrick while preaching at a youth camp one summer and was impressed with his videos and media talents. When the time came for us to fill the media minister position on staff, I contacted Alex. Though Alex was using his gifts and talents in ministry, he was not the director of media for his church. I saw a diamond in the rough. Alex came on board in 1999, and we called his brother Stephen in 2001.

God had been preparing these two from childhood to make movies. As kids they lived next door to a man who was interested in technical gadgets. He bought stop-and-go animation cameras, and Alex and Stephen used his equipment to make short videos. For years the boys put together homemade "chase 'em down and beat 'em up" movies. Later they produced commercials, movie trailers and even school projects.

All along, their parents supported them through prayer and by modeling authentic Christianity. As a result, Alex has long had a deep desire to make Christian films.

The Kendrick brothers are an asset to our staff. They have a great respect for pastoral authority and are very teachable. They have put aside egos and brotherly competition to produce movies that have made a mark on our church, on the culture and around the world. Through His sovereignty God even placed their families in the same neighborhood in Albany. This has allowed Alex and Stephen to work on story ideas or write scripts more easily.

John Hemken was the first person to have a conversation with Alex about making movies. "Ever since Alex's first interview, the idea of video really intrigued me," John said. "I remembered Michael's conversations and teachings about wanting to reach beyond the church and to touch the world from Albany, Georgia. This led to a working premise of a church existing to reach people at the point of their need (pastoral care), calling (workplace ministry), interest (small group service ideas) or inspiration (sports, education and entertainment)."

After reading an article from George Barna listing the top cultural influences, we learned that the church was sliding down the scale while movies, media and music were becoming the predominant means of influence. Since the church was listed behind sports, education and movies, we concluded we could either complain about this or address it. This mindset has been the key initiative behind the development of the Sports Park, Sherwood Christian Academy and Sherwood Pictures.

In 2001 we went to Orlando, Florida, for a staff retreat and took a day off to hang out at DisneyWorld. We took a behind-the-scenes tour and learned about their "imagineers." As we walked around the park observing the attention to detail everywhere, we were challenged with this thought: *If a secular company can be this committed to excellence, why can't the church of Jesus Christ?*

We began to think about how the church once owned the arts. The great artists of the past sculpted statues of Biblical leaders. The most exquisite masterpieces were done in the church. Many of the great songs and symphonies were composed by believers. Why had we forsaken the arts? Why were we giving creativity over to the world and the devil? Why wasn't the church on the cutting edge?

While in Orlando, John Hemken and I talked with Alex about where he wanted to be in five to ten years. He said, "I want to make movies, but no church is going to let me stay on staff and do that." I replied, "Why not? Bring me a script and a budget, and let's see if God is in it." That conversation was the genesis of Sherwood Pictures. Our goal from day one has been to make family-friendly movies that build on the Judeo-Christian ethic and communicate the gospel without compromise. We want to make movies you could take your girlfriend or your grandmother to without embarrassment.

Alex sees this move into film production as a logical extension of the church. "I think people today understand and see the world through a media filter. Almost everyone watches television. Most people see movies. Throw in the radio and the Internet, and fewer and fewer people are going inside the walls of the church to hear a pastor. I think movies are an avenue that needs to be nurtured for ministry."

How do we communicate the good news of Jesus to a Biblically illiterate and humanistic culture? How do we build churches that manifest the power and presence of God in such a way that the world notices we've been with Jesus? Traditional methods no longer seem to be effective. I grew up when the flannelgraph was cool, but that doesn't work anymore. We can either kick and scream about the situation, or we can go to work and see what God might use.

We communicate a changeless message in a changing world. We don't compromise the message, and we don't put style ahead of substance. But how do you style the substance? With clarity. This generation wants reality, transparency and honesty. Too often we've given them traditions and programs, but we've not shown them the power of God.

Alex came up with the concept for our first movie, *Flywheel*, after a staff meeting where we discussed the flywheel concept in Jim Collin's book *Good to Great*. The film was shot on location in Albany in the homes and businesses of church members. All the cast members, crew and volunteers were church members. The total cost of production was only $20,000—talk about a shoestring budget! Alex and his team shot approximately thirty-two hours of footage from November 2002 through March 2003.

By early March Alex had completed the first thirty minutes of the film except for the score. Mark Willard, our music minister, worked with Alex to compose music while they wrapped up shooting. A local theater manager granted us permission for a short run starting April 9, 2003. Stephen worked quickly to gain media exposure through our local television stations, newspaper and Chick-fil-A® restaurants.

The hard drive that housed Alex's edits was accidentally knocked off a table the last week of March, and we were heartbroken. We overnighted the drive to a repair company, but they deemed the equipment damaged beyond repair. Alex immediately began to re-edit the first thirty minutes, but it appeared that we would be unable to finish the movie by the April 9th premiere. The situation worsened when Mark's music files were lost a few days later. However, instead of calling the theater to cancel the premiere, we prayed.

> *It appeared that we would be unable to finish the movie by the April 9th premiere. However, instead of canceling, we prayed.*

During the ten days prior to the movie's release, Alex and his team continued in prayer and edited around-the-clock. A few guys loaded the raw footage and labeled it for easier editing while Mark re-recorded the music. We were down to the wire, but Alex finished the last of his edits at 6:30 a.m. on the day of the premiere. Stephen set up the projector at the local theater, and we burned the first DVD copy for the 1 p.m. showing. We were elated, but the crew was exhausted.

The 7 p.m. showing sold out the first night, and *Flywheel* was the second-highest grossing film that week. The theater asked us to extend the showings, and *Flywheel* ran for another six weeks. It was followed by a month-long run in Tifton, Georgia, and a two-week run in Columbus, Georgia.

Initially we received a few dozen emails and phone calls. Then people started accepting Christ and rededicating their lives to Him, and word spread quickly. We made 1,000 DVDs to sell in late summer 2003 and sold out the first day. We quickly ordered 2,000 more DVDs, but they were gone two weeks after they arrived. As we continued to re-order DVDs, we expected the momentum to die down, but it never did. Several websites began selling *Flywheel,* including christianfilms.com and christianmovies.com. We had reached the 10,000 mark in sales by the end of 2003.

In 2004 *Flywheel* aired on numerous Christian television networks. We walked away with seven awards from three different film festivals, including 2004 Best Screenplay at the Sabaoth International Film Festival in Milan and 2004 Best Feature at the WYSIWYG Film Festival in San Francisco. By this time we had received over 1,000 emails, and the movie was in Australia, New Zealand, Canada, South America, Europe, Romania and the Philippines.

Blockbuster video agreed to carry *Flywheel* in each of their 4,500 stores in the fall of 2004. Many other chain stores have started selling the movie, and we have sold over 85,000 units to date. We've received over 4,000 emails with testimonies of salvation decisions and rededications of fathers, mothers, businessmen, pastors, teachers and even prisoners.

Flywheel turned out to be a great tool to challenge men to step up to the plate. It's the story of a used-car salesman who is a failure at home and a crook at his business. All the while he goes to church to make business connections and keep up a religious facade; he puts empty tithe envelopes in the plate to keep up appearances. Eventually the walls start collapsing, and he turns to God in desperation. The story unfolds like a modern-day Zacheus when he begins to return what he has taken in inflated profits.

Some of our favorite stories are those from men who have made changes in their lives after being convicted of sin or dishonesty. One car salesman in Florida watched the movie and couldn't sleep that night. He saw himself as the lead character in the film and realized he was failing as a husband and father. While taking a shower the next morning he began sobbing loudly enough for his wife to hear him in the next room. He knelt on the floor of his shower and gave his life to Christ right there. Talk about getting clean before the Lord!

I believe most of us supported the idea of making a movie, but we still had our doubts. A movie by a church using all amateurs—how good can this really be? It certainly exceeded our expectations. God did exceedingly abundantly more than we ever imagined. He proved once again that if we truly dedicate something to His glory and honor, He can use it to touch and change lives in ways we'd never expect.

And the Lord had more surprises in store for us.

Production of the movie *Facing the Giants*

Setting up the car scene in *Facing the Giants*

10

Connect with the Right People

*B*Y THE TIME we began thinking about a second movie, Jim McBride had moved into the executive pastor position. I vividly recall sitting with Jim in Alex's office while Alex shared the concept and storyline for *Facing the Giants*. He was up and down, exuding passion in his eyes and voice. Jim and I sat there with tears in our eyes as we heard what God had given to Alex.

There was one major technical hitch, however. When *Flywheel* came out Alex contacted several studios that had released Christian films or low budget films about releasing our movie. All of them responded by telling us they loved the movie, but the quality was too low to be converted to film. Alex began to pray about the second movie and the need for a high definition camera that could convert to film. He asked God to give us the ability to shoot in HD. Alex began researching on the web and found the exact HD camera he wanted—the Panasonic VariCam.

In the summer of 2003 I took our creative team to Creative Outbreak Workshop, a conference started by Jay Strack with the goal of helping the church take back the arts. That week we were stretched like a rubber band by some godly creative thinkers who are making an impact in the secular world. During the conference we met David Nixon, a producer who primarily makes commercials but has done a great deal of work for Student Leadership University and Campus Crusade for Christ. While touring David's studio, Alex spotted a Panasonic VariCam, the exact camera he had been praying for. David told Alex all about the VariCam and assured him of its movie-making capabilities.

I had asked Alex to take copies of *Flywheel* to the conference in case we found a connection who would be interested in seeing it. Before leaving, Alex gave David a copy and asked him to watch it. David obliged but was skeptical of a church's cinematic abilities. He told us later that once he started watching *Flywheel* he called in his entire team to watch, and they sat glued to the screen.

A few days later David called Alex and said, "You know how to tell a story, but I know how to put together a production. If you ever do another movie, I want to help you." Alex told him about *Facing the Giants* and our need for assistance from technical professionals. David had the connections and the experience. He found four other guys who were willing to join the vision. The team came to Albany to do a boot camp and trained our laypeople to use the equipment.

David joined our team as a producer and assistant director. Originally from Australia, David has worked in the United States for the past twenty years in television and film production. Rob Whitehurst served as our location sound mixer with over twenty-five years of experience. Rob's expertise has been used on *American Idol, Cops, Sports Center* and more. Keith Slade served as lighting director, bringing a seasoned edge to the lighting elements in the movie. His work with numerous commercials, documentaries, music videos and movies was a major asset. Chip Byrd, who came on as first assistant camera, has worked on *The West Wing, Apollo 13* and much more. Chip helped us achieve a professional look, especially with the football scenes. Our director of photography, Bob Scott, had just finished shooting *Friday Night Lights* when he joined our crew. After reading the script for *Facing the Giants* he said, "I realize God has used twenty years of professional photography work to prepare me to shoot your movie."[1]

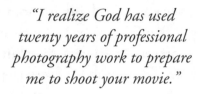

"I realize God has used twenty years of professional photography work to prepare me to shoot your movie."

"That was a huge answer to prayer," Alex said of the participation of David Nixon and his colleagues. "It was confirmation. I was asking God to do this, and boom! It happened in a way I didn't expect. From the time we got the crew together to the time the movie was released, we saw God open doors that only He could open. We were just trying to be obedient in asking the Lord to show us what to do."

While still reeling from the success of *Flywheel* and the connections God had given us through David Nixon and his team, we moved forward with our second movie project. We all had even bigger dreams in mind after God had blown us away through the success of *Flywheel*. Alex realized that God truly could do the impossible, and mere head knowledge became a conviction of the heart. We all dreamed of a mass theatrical distribution, and based on what we had seen the Lord do already, we really believed it could happen.

Alex said, "I think God looked down and said, 'Okay, this church is being obedient, and they're trying to honor Me and to do it without compromise, so I'm going to open up the doors for them.' And I have to say that it was bathed in prayer because it really was."

In *Facing the Giants* we used a football story to share the gospel. Alex and Stephen spent three months writing the script. They met in each other's homes to write each night after they put their kids to bed. We covered every aspect of the project in prayer. As we kept the church informed, the membership prayed diligently for every step along the journey.

Stephen and Alex met weekly in the prayer tower to pray over the film. Both will tell you they entered into a new level of trusting God in the process. We all did. We began to "prepare for rain" by preparing the soil of our hearts. We did everything we knew to put ourselves in a position for God to bless us, and He chose to do so. "Everyone involved in the movie was doing it with the right motives," Alex said.

We planned on a budget of $100,000 but never asked for a dime. We simply shared the need and the opportunity. Money came in small and large sums. "Praying for $20,000 for *Flywheel* seemed so big and then $100,00 for *Facing the Giants*," Alex said. "But when you commit your plans to the Lord, they will succeed."

The remarkable thing about the money coming in is that we were in the middle of the largest fund-raising effort in the history of the church. Our people were tithing, giving

love offerings, donating to missions and sacrificing to purchase land and build facilities for growth. This was not the
time to ask for money, but God provided. One couple took
Alex to lunch and gave him a check for $6,000. That same
week we received an anonymous check for $20,000.

During casting for *Facing the Giants*, we asked each person who made it to the final round of auditions if there was
anything in his or her life that potentially could prevent God's
hand of blessing from being on the film. Some people recognized unconfessed sin, harmful behaviors or sinful attitudes in their lives could be a hindrance to God's work
through the movie, and they stepped down. To the best of
our knowledge, each person cast in the film was right before
the Lord and had pure motives for wanting to be a part of
Facing the Giants.

Everyone who participated—actors, directors, technical
crews, caterers, makeup artists, set designers, security teams—
did so with a like mindset. Every detail was given over to the
Lord, and each individual used his or her talents for God's
glory alone. Everyone who volunteered to help with the film
signed an agreement stating they would not be compensated
for their work but would view their service as a gift to God.
They signed the agreement willingly and worked heartily as
unto the Lord.

The Sunday prior to shooting, we gathered as a church
family to commit the project to the Lord. Our professional
technical crew gathered at the altar as we surrounded them
and prayed over them. Alex and Stephen and all those involved stayed under the authority of the church. Because
they honored our authority, the Lord blessed our decisions
and guided us through the process.

The church was unified with the same heart and mind, and prayed fervently. As a result we saw several miracles occur on the set of the movie. One morning while shooting at Lee County High School, an electrical ballast that helped to power a massive 12,000-kilowatt light broke down. This critical piece of equipment served as our sun and moon during filming. Our lighting director was prepared to drive to Orlando to pick up another ballast from a friend, but that meant losing a few days of shooting. Discouraged and desperate, we immediately began to pray.

As soon as we finished praying someone said, "Holly is in Orlando." Holly Stiegel was our script supervisor, and her grandmother had passed away. Holly had just attended the funeral and was about to drive back to Albany at that very moment. We called her, she picked up the equipment, and in a few hours we were back to work. David Nixon's team was dumbfounded; they were used to Hollywood productions where they throw money at every problem. We didn't have money, so we had to throw prayer at every problem!

. . . Hollywood productions where they throw money at every problem. We didn't have money, so we had to throw prayer at every problem

Another God-moment occurred when we connected with Mark Richt, head football coach at the University of Georgia. Alex and Stephen thought he would be an ideal cameo for the film because of his testimony as a coach committed to faith and football. While most of us shook our heads in disbelief, Stephen called the athletic department at the school and spoke with Coach Richt's secretary.

He told her about *Facing the Giants* and asked if Mark could make a cameo appearance. She quickly declined and said he was too busy, but she allowed Stephen to send a copy of our first movie, *Flywheel*. During a one-week vacation from filming, Stephen got a call from Mark's secretary. When she gave *Flywheel* to Coach Richt he said, "Oh, I've seen this movie, and I loved it. I've watched it with my family—we laughed, we cried. I'll help these guys make this movie." It was another huge answer to prayer.

Alex and Stephen worked Coach Richt into the storyline, and we set up a time for him to come for filming. The next hurdle we faced was in getting him down to Albany. Stephen's assistant, Mandy, asked a friend's father to pick up Mark in his private plane. (It wasn't hard to persuade him—he's a University of Georgia graduate whose airplane is painted with the school colors!)

When we finished shooting the movie, Alex attended the International Christian Visual Media Conference in Atlanta. *Flywheel* was nominated for best screenplay of the year, and they also asked Alex to speak in a seminar about low-budget movie-making. After showing clips of *Flywheel* at the conference, Alex was approached by two men. They had just formed a representation company called Carmel Entertainment and asked if Alex had any other projects they could look at. Though skeptical at first, Alex gave them a rough cut of *Facing the Giants*. That turned out to be a divine appointment.

After Alex returned to Albany, he began sending rough edits to the two men from Carmel Entertainment, and they gave their critiques. Eventually they offered us a contract. We prayed diligently and cautiously agreed. Those two men, Chris Bueno and Larry Frenzel, became our representatives in seeking major theatrical distribution. They believed in our project, embraced our vision and went around talking it up in Hollywood and at other conferences.

Chris and Larry took *Facing the Giants* to 20th Century Fox, who liked the film enough to offer us a contract for DVD release. Then they took the movie to Trinity Broadcasting Network, who gave us an incredible offer for television release. We had seen God work in both of these avenues with *Flywheel,* and we were pleased to see it happen for *Facing the Giants* as well, but we longed to see a theatrical release. We reached a point where we died to that dream, convinced God had closed that door.

In August 2005 we sought permission to use a song from Third Day in *Facing the Giants.* Stephen contacted Jen King at Provident, and she asked to see the movie first. Later in the week Jen called Stephen and said, "We just saw your movie. We cried. Terry Hemmings, our president, wants to talk to you today." A few hours later Terry called Stephen and said, "We're in. We want to be part of this project. Not only can you use our songs, but we also want to help you with distribution." From that point on God resurrected our dreams and paved the way for a nationwide theatrical release.

The Rating Controversy

In May 2006 Stephen put the following request on our prayer sheet: "Pray that God will provide a breakthrough in the media that will create buzz for the movie." We were praying for that, but we never expected the "buzz" to be generated by controversy.

Two weeks later the Motion Picture Association of America announced that, due to the religious content in *Facing the Giants*, they gave the film a "PG" rating. The reaction was electric in the secular news media. A "PG" rating—for a *religious* movie?

We attracted national attention and appeared in numerous video, radio and print outlets, including *The Los Angeles Times*, *The Atlanta Journal Constitution*, CNN Headline News, Janet Parshall's America, Good Morning America and many more. The MPAA later changed their reasoning and said the rating was based on "thematic elements" such as infertility and depression. Regardless of the reasons, the "PG" rating provided the positive push we needed in the media.

The controversy escalated when House Majority Whip Roy Blunt investigated the rating and demanded further explanation from the MPAA. In an article for the *Christian Index*, Alex was quoted as follows: "I think the rating is just a sign of the times, that society does not approve of a movie that affirms a Christian belief system. At first we were a little surprised at the ruling, but we believe that God is go-

> *God was glorified, and we probably gained millions of dollars worth of free advertisement out of the "controversy."*

ing to use this for his glory."[1] God was glorified, and we probably gained millions of dollars worth of free advertising out of the "controversy." We can now say with Joseph, "You meant this for evil, but God meant it for good" (Gen. 50:20).

During my first trip to New York to appear on the FOX News Network, I did a seven-minute interview with a live studio audience. We closed with a "question and answer" time, and I wasn't sure what to expect from the crowd. By His grace God put a pastor and a Christian coach in the audience to ask questions. During our first national network news experience, God showed Himself strong on our behalf. As we left the studio and stood on Broadway, I said to Alex, "Just think: there are millions of people on this island, and not one of them is going to stop and ask us for an autograph. If we can keep the perspective that we are servants of God and not celebrities, God might use this." Most people in this world won't know or care that we've made a movie, but God has given us an opportunity to touch people's lives.

We've also received our share of unexpected reactions. I was on a radio show that covered Virginia and the Carolinas to talk about how we made *Facing the Giants*. Prior to call-in I talked about working with Provident to use the song from Third Day because the movie is targeted at a youth culture. I mentioned that we had used music from Third Day, Casting Crowns and other contemporary Christian artists in the film. The last caller was a pastor from the Carolinas. He said in a judgmental tone, "You mentioned something about Third Day and Casting Crowns. That sounds a whole lot like *that* contemporary Christian music."

I explained to him that we knew about all the artists, and the songs had a clear Christian message. He replied, "Well, I think you would have done a whole lot better if your music had been the old stuff like 'Rock of Ages.'"

I love "Rock of Ages." It's a great song. I grew up singing it, but I don't know how it fits into a football movie. I further explained to the pastor that we had seen 187 people come to Christ in screenings in Boston and New York. He replied, "Many call him Lord, Lord and do not the things He says."

There are some people you can never satisfy. I'm glad we listened to the voice of God and not the voices of men.

The movie opened on September 29, 2006, in 441 screens from Tampa to Anchorage. When it finished its seventeen-week theatrical run, *Facing the Giants* had been in 1,010 screens and grossed over ten million dollars.

Sony released the DVD in January 2007. It has been produced with audio and/or subtitles in ten languages—English, Spanish, Portuguese, French, Thai, Mandarin Chinese, Hindi, Arabic, Dutch and Italian—and more are in process. The DVD has been released in fifty-six countries and is being sold on every continent around the globe The impact has spread beyond our ability to comprehend.

We have seen God accomplish the impossible in our midst. We have stood in amazement as He worked miracles before our eyes. We have watched Sherwood Baptist Church *literally* touch the world from Albany, Georgia.

I asked a few people involved with the film to share their own comments on this experience.

"When I am clean before God and stay in prayer, it's almost exponential what He does. When I'm in my flesh or I'm doing something from a selfish motive, the fruit is logical—there's nothing phenomenal about it. The same is true for the whole group who made this movie. When you're prayed up and right before Him, and you're taking those steps of faith, it's exponential. We started thinking fifteen theaters in Atlanta then forty theaters to cover Georgia. We ended up with an initial release in 441 theaters and eventually 1,010 altogether. It makes me laugh. I never would have imagined it."

— *Alex Kendrick*

"When you pray according to heaven's agenda, God answers those prayers. We prayed, 'Lord will You help us reach people for Christ? Will You help us edify the church? Will You help us take the gospel to the ends of the earth? Would You be glorified through this process?' Our goals were not to make money, become famous and brag on ourselves."

— *Stephen Kendrick*

"One of the greatest takeaways has been interacting with the body of Christ across the country. Those experiences have expanded my vision. We aren't the only group. We've seen so many people across this nation with their hands to the plow, trying to make an impact for Christ. Thinking back on all those faces provides great consolation on days when the enemy seeks to discourage us."

— *Jim McBride*

11

Send the Rain

*M*OST PEOPLE only know about Sherwood because of our movies. Some might think that's all we've done. In reality it's only a slice of a much larger pie. A few years ago our people bought into the vision for a conference called ReFRESH, a time of spiritual renewal and revival. We've experienced some God-moments in this annual meeting that cannot be orchestrated.

Ron Dunn had been speaking for years at our annual Bible conference, but when he passed away in 2001, I wasn't sure what to do. I knew I wanted to continue to set aside four days every September for a concentrated emphasis, but I didn't know what direction to take. God began to stir in my heart a desire for a conference focused on revival and awakening.

Our first ReFRESH Conference was held in 2003. Our guest speaker was evangelist Bill Stafford, who has preached at Bible conferences and pastors' conferences around the world. He is a leader in the ministry of revival to pastors and churches in many parts of the globe.

During the weeks prior to the conference, I preached on revival. One Sunday night I taught about the woman with the issue of blood (Mark 5:25–34). Jesus was on His way to the house of Jairus as people followed Him in great numbers. In the middle of that crowd was a woman who had suffered severely. She was destitute from all her medical bills, had an incurable disease and was ceremonially unclean— but she possessed the kind of desperation God is looking for. She resolved in her heart, "I've got to get through to Jesus. I must see Him and touch Him." There was holy desperation in her act.

She was not only desperate; she was willing to act in faith. She believed if she could get through to Jesus, she would be made whole. She was willing to use what little energy she had left to press through the crowd, to risk condemnation from the Pharisees and rebuke from the cynics. She worked her way through the multitude, touched the hem of His garment and was made new.

Throughout the Gospels we see that Jesus was attracted to desperate people. He healed the lame man after his friends went to the extreme of lowering him through the roof of the house (Mark 2:1–12). He gave sight to blind Bartimaeus who would not listen to those who told him to be quiet and leave the Master alone (Mark 10:46–52).

> *Throughout the Gospels we see that Jesus was attracted to desperate people.*

We often fail to press through the obstacles and opposition to get to Jesus. We worry about what others will think or about not having enough faith. We cave in to our feelings. We believe our doubts and doubt our faith.

Too many churches and leaders resemble the rich young ruler. They aren't desperate. They want life on their terms. They don't want to be inconvenienced by the cross. Like the church in Revelation, they are rich and in need of nothing. No man can be a true disciple until he is willing to receive instruction. No church can make an impact until it is willing to get to Jesus no matter the cost. As long as we lean on our own understanding, we'll only have a ministry of flesh, wood, hay and stubble.

The woman pressed through. She touched Jesus. Our Lord immediately stopped and asked, "Who touched Me?" The disciples must have thought that was a dumb question! How could Jesus ask that with a crowd of people pressing in around Him? But as Vance Havner said, "Many were thronging Jesus, but only one touched Him."[1]

People push and shove to gain an edge, even using Jesus to their advantage. They treat the Lord like a bellhop or an ecclesiastical Santa Claus. Few touch Him. The reason we have not seen revival in our lifetime is we've failed to be desperate. If it's not convenient we aren't interested. Vance Havner said,

> We sit in church, we listen, but we are not overwhelmed with urgency and emergency. The whole matter is one we can take or leave. We are leaning on other things; we have not reached extremity. So we do not touch Him, and consequently, His power does not go out into our lives and we go away empty, while some poor, wretched soul, driven to desperation, simply touches the hem of His garment and is made whole.[2]

The crowd will never push for revival. Only the remnant is interested in revival. Revival is an inconvenient interruption for the status quo. It is an admission of sin and shortcoming. It is a time of repentance that leads to refreshing. We want Living Water, but we don't want to get off the couch to drink deeply of it.

When I finished preaching from Mark 5 that night prior to our first ReFRESH conference, the glory fell. The invitation went nearly two hours. Parents went to the nursery and brought their children to the altar to pray over them. People who were suffering physically and others who had prodigal children found themselves surrounded by people praying for them. None of this was driven or orchestrated from the platform.

After the service I stood in the center aisle exhausted and exhilarated. I told the staff they needed to place memorial stones down on this date and tell their children about it in the future. Most ministers can serve for fifty years and never see a service like that one—and the best was yet to come. As I walked out of the service that night, I embraced one of our ushers, Ray Wood. (Ray plays the character of Mr. Bridges in *Facing the Giants*.) I began praying with him and cried out, "God, You promised. God, You promised, and it only takes one."

Ray says he didn't sleep that night but was up crying out and praying to the Lord. In fact, that same routine continued for the next several nights. On Wednesday Ray came by my office to say that he couldn't get over what had happened on Sunday night. We prayed together, and I agreed to let Ray share his testimony the following Sunday. At 3:30 Friday morning God laid a message on Ray's heart. When I saw him again on the Sunday he was scheduled to speak, I asked Ray, "Are you ready?" He said, "If the words that come from my lips are His words and not mine, the altar and the aisles will be filled."

That night, September 7, 2003, Ray shared his testimony. He also spoke from Genesis 18, where Abraham pleads with God to spare the cities of Sodom and Gomorrah. In closing, Ray spoke these words of desperation over the congregation:

Lord, if You could move among this people, and if You could find fifty hearts that were broken, that would come and bow before You, Lord, would You send Your glory? Lord, if You could only find forty broken hearts in this people that would bow down before You, Lord, would You bring down Your glory and fill this room? Lord, do not be mad, I ask this one more time. Lord, if there's only thirty that You can find in this room with broken hearts, Lord, will You come down in Your glory and Your power? Lord, I ask You, if You could just find twenty with broken hearts that would come and bow before You would You fill this place with Your power and Your glory? Lord, I am but ashes and trash before Your eyes, but I ask You, Lord, if You could just find ten with broken hearts that would come down and bow before You, would You fill this place with Your power and glory? Lord, I'm broken and poured out before You, and I ask You, Lord, restore me. Bring revival into my life. Lord, I love You and I praise You.

When Ray finished speaking a silence fell over the room as men, women and children lined the altar and the aisles on their knees. After a short time I began reading from Romans 8:

For those who are according to the flesh set their minds on the things of the flesh, but those who are according to the Spirit, the things of the Spirit. For the mind set on the flesh is death, but the mind set on the Spirit is life and peace, because the mind set on the flesh is hostile toward God; for it does not subject itself to the law of God, for it is not even able to do so; and those who are in the flesh cannot please God. However, you are not in the flesh but in the Spirit, if indeed the Spirit of God dwells in you. But if anyone does not have the Spirit of Christ, he does not belong to Him. And if Christ is in you, though the body is dead because of sin, yet the spirit is alive because of righteousness. . . . And in the same way the Spirit also helps our weakness; for we do not know how to pray as we should, but the Spirit Himself intercedes for us with groanings too deep for words; and He who searches the hearts knows what the mind of the Spirit is, because He intercedes for the saints according to the will of God. And we know that God causes all things to work together for good to those who love God, to those who are called according to His purpose. . . . What then shall we say to these things? If God is for us, who is against us? He who did not spare His own Son, but delivered Him up for us all, how will He not also with Him freely give us all things? . . . But in all these things we overwhelmingly conquer through Him who loved us. For I am convinced that neither death, nor life, nor angels, nor principalities, nor things present, nor things to come, nor powers, nor height, nor depth, nor any other created thing, shall be able to separate us from the love of God, which is in Christ Jesus our Lord. (Rom. 8:5–10, 26–28, 31–32, 37–39)

God had moved among us in power, and we were overwhelmed. Some stood, many knelt. Some prayed in silence while others wept in repentance. After singing together for a while, I invited Linda Breland, wife of Roger Breland, to close us in prayer. Linda is one of the greatest prayer warriors I know. She understands how to get hold of God. In tenderness and humility she prayed:

> *God had moved among us in power, and we were overwhelmed. Some stood, many knelt. Some prayed in silence while others wept in repentance.*

> Father, we humble ourselves in Your presence. We bow down before You in submission to Your authority, Your will, Your power, Your presence and Your hand in our lives. We thank You for bringing each one of us to this moment, this moment of truth, when we choose to go with You whether none goes with us. I pray over every man and woman, young person and child in this room tonight. I pray that You'll have Your will and Your way in each one of us, and that none of us will turn from You, or excuse our sin, or go our own way. Thank You, Father, for Your mercy that endures forever. Thank You for Your grace that You pour out on those who choose to be humble. Lord, we pray like Moses did. Father, will You show us Your glory? Will You show us Your ways? Not just the acts, Your miracles, but would You be so intimate with us that we understand Your ways?

We all left that night with a greater sense of expectation about what God would do in our midst during the conference. Throughout the week of ReFRESH, one moment stands out in my mind among several. John Dees is a key figure in our church. He is a man of influence, yet humble and gracious. John joined the church at age twelve and was baptized. The more he came to church and listened to the Word preached and taught, the more he knew he had never received Christ as his Savior.

John was convicted to make things right with the Lord regarding his baptism after salvation. There had been other times when he had wanted to make a new commitment to Christ and be baptized, but because he had served as a deacon and in other areas of ministry in the church, he never had the nerve to follow through. After Bill Stafford's message one evening during ReFRESH, John walked to the altar and expressed his need to be baptized on the right side of his salvation. I later had the privilege of baptizing my dear friend.

In the six or seven weeks following ReFRESH, we baptized eighty people who either realized they had never trusted Christ or had trusted Christ after their baptism. They wanted to get things right with God. In a prayer environment like ReFRESH, there was freedom from worrying about other people's perceptions. God peeled back the hypocrisy and drew many people to Himself.

When the conference was "over," I felt compelled to continue the meetings. We gathered for the next two weeks to pray, seek the Lord and stay in the flow of what God was doing. On Thursday the revival spilled over to our high school campus. Some students were getting right with God and one another while other students were coming to Christ as Lord and Savior.

My wife headed the drama department at the school

during that time. She arrived to find students huddled in the cafeteria praying and repenting. During the last few hours of school, teachers began to notice some of their students weren't in class who had been at school earlier that day. Slowly word began to trickle through the school that students were gathering in the cafeteria for prayer and singing.

Over the next few hours students and teachers congregated in the cafeteria, circled around the outside walls. They sang and prayed together. In the midst of that environment, one senior girl walked across the room to three other senior girls on the other side. She told them she had been in school with them for a number of years and had always treated them as inferior. The Lord showed her that her life itself was like filthy rags. She sought their forgiveness right there in front of all her peers.

Her actions sparked similar scenarios across the room. Teachers and students shared tears, restored fellowships and renewed friendships. The revival continued on after school and flowed over into the next school day. Administrators even suspended some classes due to God's Spirit moving so powerfully throughout the campus. The revival scene on the football field in *Facing the Giants* is a direct reflection of what happened at Sherwood Christian Academy.

Teachers and students shared tears, restored fellowships and renewed friendships. The revival continued on after school and flowed over into the next school day.

In 2004 Bill Stafford, Ken Jenkins and I were the keynote speakers at ReFRESH. Ken is a godly layman who is a wildlife and nature photographer. Ken's pictures have been used by *National Geographic* and other wildlife publications across the country. He has a phenomenal ministry of using his photography to reveal great truths about God. His work makes you reflect and go deeper with God.

When the last service was over that year, Ken, Bill and I (almost in one voice) said it was time to expand the conference. We determined to take the conference to the Smokey Mountains and concentrate on influencing pastors. My heart's desire is to impact, influence, encourage and exhort pastors to seek the Lord for personal and corporate revival.

In 2005 we had our first conference in Pigeon Forge, Tennessee. I had hoped for three hundred; we had twenty-six. Still, God was with us, and we determined to press on. The following year we had forty-six attendees. At this point I wondered if this really was a God-idea or just a good idea. I seriously considered canceling the conference, as it required a great deal of work on top of our already busy schedules.

But God would not release me. When we first started the conference, we were told it would take three years to establish the name and the event. By the grace of God some donors came forward to invest in ReFRESH in the Smokies and to help us pay the bills. We operated on a lean budget with almost no funds for advertising.

We turned the corner in 2007, a very pivotal year for us. One pastor and staff member who had attended in 2006 brought thirty-eight people with them. We had funds to scholarship some church planters and pastors who had no budget for conferences. The conference drew 142 people, and thirty-two of those were pastors. During registration this year we gave every attendee a packet of prayer cards written by our members. We assigned every pastor to a Sherwood member who would host him for lunch on the first day of the conference. Several couples from Sherwood attended at their own expense and hosted these pastors for a meal and prayed for them.

We found that many pastors came to the conference exhausted. They were out of gas, and the flow was down to a trickle. By the end of the three days I saw men with renewed energy and passion. Let me share with you a few of their comments:

It was glorious being in the mountains of Tennessee all week, listening and being fed by men of God who want more than anything to experience revival in their own lives and in the lives of their churches. There was a sweet spirit that pervaded every session, and we knew God's presence was there among us. What was it that made this one unlike any of the other conferences that I have attended? Everyone was in one accord, and there was humility in every person that we talked to. Grace abounded from each man and woman that we came in contact with. We all wanted the same thing: a touch from God. We wanted to be different when we left the meeting, different from the way we had come.

—Music Minister, Florida

I have been to a lot of conferences, but I can honestly say that this was the best yet. The emphasis on revival and spiritual awakening was just what I needed. I did not get the sense that any of the speakers were trying to impress anyone, but rather, that they were simply seeking God's will for each of us. The setting allowed the opportunity to get away from daily concerns at home and really focus on the Lord Jesus Christ.

—Senior Pastor, Georgia

Thank you for the ReFRESH Conference. The entire event was excellent. The sacrifice that you, your staff and church family made was overwhelming. Each time the Word was delivered, I felt that the power of God was being displayed. Thank you for an organized event that was sensitive to the leading of the Holy Spirit. Your willingness to invest in others has made a difference in my life and ministry. I left ReFRESH with a renewed passion to lead our church to invest in other people and other faithful servants.

–Senior Pastor, Georgia

We left Tennessee, but we have not left the mountaintop experience of the ReFRESH Conference. Everything about the week was God-breathed. When the members of our church checked in and were given the cards from the prayer team at Sherwood, so many of them asked me if I had discussed their needs with you or another member of your church. God, in a way that only He can orchestrate, matched the needs of our members with the prayers of your members. We experienced one God-moment after another. All of the men that were there to speak to us had messages that ministered to every one of our members. Some fell under great conviction, and one lady shared this past Sunday night as she wept, "I am not the same person that went to the conference." God bless you for having the heart for pastors that you do. Please thank the members of Sherwood Baptist for being the church that God is using to change the world from Albany, Georgia.

–Staff Member, Florida

Part of the ministry of Sherwood is to pastors. We love ministers and want to invest in their lives. Through the Ron Dunn Center on our campus, we are training seminary students at the New Orleans Baptist Theological Seminary extension. Through ReFRESH and Bridge Builders (a conference that brings together pastors of different races and cultures), we are seeking to stop the bleeding in some wounded men of God. We believe God is the friend of wounded hearts. He has compassion for the brokenhearted and strength for those who are weary in well-doing.

> *We believe God is the friend of wounded hearts. He has compassion for the brokenhearted and strength for those who are weary in well-doing.*

Most of the men we minister to are not from large churches. They probably will never be written about in their denominational magazines. They may never be called on to speak at a state or national convention. We believe there are no big preachers or small preachers, just preachers. There are no big churches or small churches, just churches. The greatest and hardest work of all may be the pastorate of a country church.

Not only do we want to impact the culture, we also want to impact churches. We want to help pastors and staff members. We continue to seek the Lord and pray for financial support for ReFRESH because we believe this is something we will eventually do in several locations around the country.

We want to give pastors the personal touch. They can go to conferences that sound like a preaching competition where one guy is trying to out-preach the next guy. Rarely in a large conference do you get to rub shoulders with the speakers. We intentionally keep ReFRESH small so we can keep the personal touch aspect alive.

While working on this book, a bi-vocational pastor, Robert Spurgeon (yes, he is a descendant of Charles Spurgeon and bears a remarkable resemblance), called my office. He pastors a church with an average attendance of one hundred. He returned home from ReFRESH in the Smokies and shared with his congregation what God had done in his heart. During the invitation at least thirty of his members were at the altar weeping and getting right with God. I wept as he told me. Just hearing his story makes me want to do more to touch the lives of pastors and churches.

The fullness of the Spirit and a season of revival is not a "press the button" panacea. It is the growing experience of a heart hungry for God and dissatisfied with business as usual. At our conferences we don't try to organize a revival. We do try to set our sails to catch the wind of the Spirit. Revival comes by agonizing, not organizing.

Revival is a divine interruption. I long for something to happen that is not on our planned-out, pre-arranged calendars. In 1975 I heard James Baker Cauthen say, "We're so organized and planned out that if the Holy Spirit left we could run for ten years and never know He was gone." We don't have time to seek God because we have to sell the latest product.

Revivals were never intended to last. Feelings will wane. Emotions will die down. Billy Sunday said, "They tell me a revival is only temporary; so is a bath, but it does one good."[3] The results of revival can endure. Vance Havner said, "There never was a real revival that did not produce heartburn and hallelujahs."[4] It will weed out a crowd, prune the church, purify the Body and advertise itself. Churches have held revivals, but someone needs to turn one loose and let God do His own thing in our midst.

If we are going to have revival or see another Great Awakening in our lifetime, we have to start preparing our fields and praying for rain. We must become desperate for God. The sovereignty of God does not eliminate or negate our responsibility to get before God. It does mean we can boldly approach the throne of grace. God desires for His people to be revived more than we can imagine.

We can no longer allow our prayer meetings to be for physical needs only. C. S. Lewis said, "It is quite useless knocking at the door of heaven for earthly comfort; it's not the sort of comfort they supply there."[5] Our problems are spiritual. Our needs are spiritual. The solutions are not fleshly; they are spiritual. We will not overcome spiritual darkness with fleshly efforts, no matter how sincere we are.

Because God set His heart on us, it is only right for us to set our hearts on Him. Loving God with all our hearts is the key. Passionate obedience to God is a non-negotiable. One of the most famous statements from the lips of our Lord is found in the seventh chapter of John's Gospel:

> Now on the last day, the great day of the feast, Jesus stood and cried out, saying, "If anyone is thirsty, let him come to Me and drink. He who believes in Me, as the Scripture said, 'From his innermost being will flow rivers of living water.'" But this He spoke of the Spirit, whom those who believed in Him were to receive; for the Spirit was not yet given, because Jesus was not yet glorified. (7:37–39)

Warren Wiersbe writes:

> The last day of the feast would be the seventh day, a very special day on which the priests would march seven times around the altar, chanting Psalm 118:25. . . . No doubt

just as they were pouring out the water, symbolic of the water Moses drew from the rock, Jesus stood and shouted His great invitation to thirsty sinners.

It has been pointed out that this "great day," the twenty-first of the seventh month, is the same date on which the Prophet Haggai made a special prediction about the temple (Hag. 2:1–9). . . . Haggai 2:6–7 is quoted in Hebrews 12:26–29 as applying to the return of the Lord.

Jesus was referring to the experience of Israel recorded in Exodus 17:1–7. That water was but a picture of the Spirit of God. Believers would not only drink the living water, but they would become channels of living water to bless a thirsty world! The "artesian well" that He promised in John 4:14 has now become a flowing river!

Water for drinking is one of the symbols of the Holy Spirit in the Bible. (Water for washing is a symbol of the Word of God; see John 15:3 and Eph. 5:26.) Just as water satisfies thirst and produces fruitfulness, so the Spirit of God satisfies the inner person and enables us to bear fruit. At the feast, the Jews were reenacting a tradition that could never satisfy the heart. Jesus offered them living water and eternal satisfaction![6]

Are you thirsty? Are you in a rut? Are you thinking about quitting? Come to Jesus, the source of Living Water. We will not find water that satisfies in religion, programs or events. It's only found in the person of Jesus Christ. It's not a magic formula. What He has done for others He will do for you. Are you willing to believe God for that? Are you willing to push aside the secondary and focus on the primary?

Remove the giants of fear from your life. Don't focus on the obstacles; focus on the opportunities. Ask God to do a fresh work in your heart. Read books about the history of revival, and ask God to do it again. Ask Him to start in you. Prepare your heart to receive a refreshing from the Lord. Prepare for rain—plow your field and believe God for a harvest. There just might be a rain cloud on your horizon.

Prayer during the 2003 ReFRESH Conference

ReFRESH in the Smokies, Pigeon Forge,Tennesse

12

That's a Wrap

*W*E'VE RECEIVED thousands of emails. We know of over 3,000 people who have put their trust in Christ as Lord and Savior after seeing *Facing the Giants*. We've heard from many football teams that had losing records who turned their seasons around after seeing the film and went on to win their state championships. Some have said the movie is not believable. Tell that to those whose lives have been changed and to the losers who became winners.

We know of a number of colleges that watched the film before playing in major games. We know of three major college upsets that happened the Saturday after the team watched the film. One college picked up a phrase from the movie, "Stone Wall!" for their defense. We have pictures from teams whose cheerleaders designed run-through banners that said, "Stone Wall" or "Prepare for Rain."

We could spend the rest of our lives debating over methods. The truth is that we all know we're sinners saved by

God's grace, and this world needs to know Jesus. The question is: Are we doing anything about it? Or do we spend our time complaining about the culture? Some people think you can be holy by crawling in a hole, but Jesus didn't call us to hide from the world. He called us out of the world so we could go back in it and be salt and light.

Jim McBride attended a screening in Washington, D.C. A pastor there said, "Movies are the stained glass windows of the 21st century." If you look at the old cathedrals of Europe, you can walk in the room, and the windows tell a story. Jesus told stories and taught the masses in parables. As I heard the late Frederick Samson say, "Who am I to try to improve on my Master's method?" Jesus told stories that touched the hearts of people. What are you doing to share that story with the world around you?

There are more ways to do ministry than just preaching and teaching Sunday school. We all have to get alone with God and find out what He has called us to do. What are you believing God for? It doesn't have to big and bombastic. It doesn't have to make the front page of the newspaper. Jesus quietly went about His business. He didn't teach and preach like the Pharisees; he stood above religion. Jesus hurt with people and wept for a city. What are we doing as the body of Christ to show the humanity of Jesus?

We all have to get alone with God and find out what He has called us to do. What are you believing God for?

Too often we perform in order to receive applause or a

pat on the back. Sometimes this kind of ministry means the left hand doesn't know what the right hand is doing. People followed Jesus because of His authenticity. Authenticity and consistency are a big deal. We've had numerous people visit Sherwood nearly every week because of *Facing the Giants.* My prayer is that the perception that attracted them to visit would be matched with reality. We must be spiritually authentic, not a cheap replica of another church. We're not doing bad impersonations of one another; we're to be original and unique.

Just like the movie says, when we're fleshing out God's plans for our life or our church, our fear often collides with our faith. Too often people see the obstacles instead of the opportunities, and thus fail to attempt anything at all. William Carey said, "Attempt great things *for* God; expect great things *from* God."

When the disciples witnessed Jesus walking on the water, they were terrified. But Jesus told them not to be afraid and invited Peter to step out of the boat onto the water. Peter got out of the boat and began walking, but became afraid and started sinking. It was only the hand of Jesus that kept him from drowning (see Matthew 14:22–33). Peter's fear and faith collided.

What do you do when your faith collides with fear? How do press on and accomplish all that God has planned for your life?

The first thing to remember is, never let a loser tell you how to win. You will always have people tell you why you can't do something great for God. The world is full of dissenters, complainers and skeptics. You will probably be faced with excuses like:

"We've tried that before."   "That's not our problem."

"It can't be done."   "You're right, but . . ."

"It won't work."   "Why change?"

"You're too radical."   "I like things the way they are."

"It's not practical."   "We aren't ready."

"Let's be reasonable."   "We don't have the money."

There is too much work to be done. We don't have time to orchestrate ministry on the whims of carnal people who only know two words: "no" and "can't." Peter didn't allow the other disciples in the boat to stop him from stepping out on the water. They may have laughed or called him "crazy," but he didn't listen.

Secondly, look beyond the obstacles and circumstances around you. The wind did what the disciples couldn't do—it got Peter's eyes off of Jesus. We can't see the wind, but we can see its effects. Instead of glancing at the circumstances and gazing at the Master, Peter glanced at the Master and gazed at the circumstances. Unfortunately, the circumstances will rarely be completely favorable for believing God. We're forced to believe God in darkness, crisis, tragedy, grief, suffering and uncertainty. Have you ever considered the following:

- Alexander the Great conquered the world by his thirtieth birthday but never went to college.

- Shakespeare was one of the greatest writers in history, but he didn't know how to type.

- Knute Rockne, a legendary coach at Notre Dame, never won an NCAA championship.

- The twelve disciples never had a best-selling book or renowned religious talk show.

- Paul was never voted *TIME Magazine's* "Man of the Year."

- Martin Luther was considered a heretic by his peers.

- John Bunyan wrote *Pilgrim's Progress* in prison.

- A church in Albany, Georgia, made a movie!

Circumstances will change, but God is constant. James tells us that with the Father "there is no variation, or shifting shadow" (1:17). In a world of instability and insecurity, place your hope in One who is forever stable and secure.

Thirdly, realize that you can't walk by faith in your flesh. Matthew 14:29 tells us that Jesus responded to Peter's request to get out of the boat by saying, "Come." Don't get out of the boat until Jesus says to. When He says, "Come," then make your move. The right thing at the wrong time is the wrong thing. Timing is essential for us to see God's blessings. I thought Sherwood was ready to build a new facility in 1992; we didn't build until 2000. I wanted to change our worship style in 1990; we made gradual changes over a five-year period without a fight or a split. We finished filming *Facing the Giants* in 2004, yet had to wait until 2006 for national distribution. Be patient, wait on the Lord and trust His timing.

Finally, get out of the boat! Peter would have never walked on water had he stayed in the comfort of the boat. It is always safer on the water with Jesus than it is in the boat without Him. Jesus didn't rebuke Peter for stepping out of the boat in faith. He rebuked Peter for losing his focus while concentrating on the circumstances. Very

> *Peter would never have walked on water had he stayed in the comfort of the boat.*

few people ever accomplish their dreams. They craft grandiose plans, but never overcome their fear to step out of the boat. You've read the story of a church that attempted the impossible. Our prayer is that God would use our steps of faith to challenge you or your church to do the same.

There comes a time when we must seize the opportunity. We've talked enough. It's time to get out of the boat. Ron Dunn has a great story about how faith must lead to action:

> Let's imagine that we are driving through a rural area and we stop at a farmhouse. Sitting on the front porch, rocking slowly back and forth in an ancient rocker, is the farmer.
>
> "What are you doing?" we ask.
>
> "Farming," he says.
>
> "What are you growing?"
>
> "Wheat."
>
> But as we look out over his fields we see nothing but unploughed and unplanted ground. "Excuse us, sir," we say, "but you haven't ploughed your fields. And it doesn't look like you've planted any wheat."
>
> "Yes, that's right."
>
> "We don't understand."
>
> "I'm farming by faith. Believing God for a crop."
>
> "But," we protest, "shouldn't you be *doing* something— maybe planting some wheat?"
>
> "I *am* doing something," he says.
>
> "What?"
>
> "I'm praying. Praying and believing. Praise the Lord!"
>
> If every farmer exercised that kind of faith we would all have starved to death long ago. But that is no more ridiculous than some of the ideas about faith floating around. There is something we must do. Abiding in the Lord is not *idling* in the Lord. Faith must express itself by working.[1]

Outside the Box? What Box?

It has been said that we're a church that "thinks outside the box." Have you ever thought about what that implies? Boxes are meant for packing and shipping—to keep things contained and protected, so they can be put to use at some other time in some other place. They have labels on them like "This Side Up" or "Fragile." They are stuffed with packing materials to keep the items from moving around. Maybe our problem is we've allowed people to put us in a box in our lives and ministries. We've believed our critics and the cynics and not heard the voice of God calling us to follow Him.

You know what I've found? *There is no box!* The only boundaries are the Word of God and the will of God, and the Spirit of God is totally capable of keeping me within His parameters. Think how different the world would be if Martin Luther, George Müeller, Watchman Nee, Jonathan Edwards and others had said, "We can't do that, the system won't allow it."

If you are in a box, get out! Find out what He has called you to do and stay there long enough to see it happen. Seek the Lord, plow up your fallow ground until He comes and rains down righteousness on you. Ask God to give you the faith and tenacity to prepare for a harvest. Believe God for a harvest even if there seems to be no chance of a coming shower of blessing.

It's not an easy journey; I have the battle scars to prove it. There are days when you might want to quit. But I can tell you without reservation that when you see the rain coming, when you stand drenched in his blessings, when God does it in such a way that only He can get the glory, it's worth every pain, prayer, setback and valley.

I would love to hear of the things God is doing with you and your ministry as you prepare for rain. Contact me at:

Michael Catt
2201 Whispering Pines Road
Sherwood Baptist Church
Albany, Ga. 31707
www.sherwoodbaptist.net
michaelc@sherwoodbaptist.net

— — — — —

www.2ProphetU.com
A free web resource started by Michael Catt and Warren Wiersbe to encourage and challenge pastors and ministers in their ministry.

— — — — —

ReFRESH
Conference

www.ReFRESHConference.org
Conferences designed to refresh believers and call the remnant to seek the Lord for revival.

— — — — —

www.vancehavner.com
A web site created to provide information on the life and ministry of Vance Havner.

From Our Inbox . . .

Excerpts from emails received about *Facing the Giants*

(From a father and high school science teacher
in South Carolina)

Tonight I had the opportunity to see *Facing the Giants*.
Thank you for your courage and faith in God in this project.
. . .

In October of 2005, my wife, mother and father-in-law,
and grandmother-in-law were all killed in a car wreck. . . . As
a result, I am a single dad with three children, ages sixteen,
five and two-and-a-half.

Thank you so much for your work in *Facing the Giants*.
It's so applicable on so, so many levels. It wasn't just about
football. It wasn't just about Sherwood. It's about facing challenges and relying on God's strength and His power. When
my wife was killed, I realized that I had absolutely nowhere
to go. No one on this planet had any clue how to give me
any type of peace, but God did. I still grieve daily. I will
probably continue to grieve for some time. But my children know that their Mommy and grandparents are in
heaven waiting on us. My children know that Jesus is com-

ing back and soon we'll all be in heaven in the presence of Jesus. My children learned that in church and at home.

(From a soldier on his second tour of duty in Iraq)

Hello from Baghdad, Iraq. . . . I grew up attending a Baptist church, but after I joined the Army I began living for myself and not for God. In July I deployed to Iraq for the second time in three years. . . On my satellite TV system I stumbled across a special on the making of your movie and I was moved. Not only in my loneliness did I find a piece of home (the South) but by the fact that so many people put so much time and effort into this movie not for profit or gain but to uplift God. Well to make a long story short, I have rededicated my life to God and long to grow closer to Him every day. I cannot say why I happened across that channel on that day but I thank God for leading me there. I wish you the best in your outreach program and include you in my prayers every day. My only regret is that I will probably never see the movie as I will be in Iraq until July 2007. . . . Thanks again for all that you do and your continued support of all the troops deployed.

(A later email from the same soldier)

I had a friend send me a copy of the movie—yes, all the way from NY—and I was so moved by the whole product. Even being here in Iraq and having lost over 50 soldiers from our unit thus far and with two still missing, I thank God every day for allowing me to serve him and my country. Your movie was such an inspiration and blessing that I have passed it around to all as a way to minister to them. To date there have been six of my brothers in arms who are now brothers in Christ. May God continue to bless you and your outreach. Please pass my thanks to all of the kind folks back there for their continued support and prayers for all of the men and women here. I can testify that they are not being unheard.

(From a woman working in a prison ministry)

I wanted to personally write and thank you for having the vision and making the movie, *Facing the Giants*. I know that it was God-led and a wonderful collaborative effort from your entire church. I had heard of the movie from my pastor and others that had seen it and loved it. My personal desire to watch the movie came from the women at our local jail. Every weekend the officers at the jail choose a movie from their collection to show the inmates. It is broadcast on all the TV sets in every "pod" therefore it is hard for everyone in the jail to not see the chosen movie. The jail staff has agreed to show Christian movies if they have them. Your movie made an incredible impact on the ladies that I minister to on Sunday nights. They had so many questions about the Lord the Sunday after seeing the movie. It was amazing! I watched the movie last night so that when I go into the jail in a couple of hours I will be prepared to discuss any questions about our loving Father that they have from *Facing the Giants*. The women that I see are facing some HUGE giants (drug addition, sexual issues, broken families, etc.). It was inspirational for them to see a film that showed the power of prayer and the love of our God! I cannot thank your church enough for making a movie that reaches so many people in all walks of life. Praise to the King of Kings!

(From a football coach at a Christian high school)

We watched *Facing the Giants* on the trip to the state championship game. The boys, to say the least, were ready to go do their best for the God they serve, win or lose. The game, as you can tell by the score (68-18), went well. At the end of the contest, the boys, parents, and coaches were all praising God and giving glory to Him for delivering the victory. Both teams circled up and prayed and thanked Him for the opportunity to play in such a memorable game.

Guess what the boys wanted to watch on the way back? You guessed it—*Facing the Giants*.

I can't express my gratitude enough for what you did to make this happen. You all were instrumental in the spiritual high our team was on. Thanks again and may God continue to bless your ministry and your efforts to reach the world.

(From a father who had just gone through a difficult divorce and is struggling with anger)

. . . When the movie got to the point where the coach blind-folded the player and started yelling DON'T QUIT, I lost it and had to stop the movie while I wept. At that point I realized I had quit on God and was ashamed of myself for being so selfish. I watched the rest of the movie in and out of tears. This movie has touched me more than any movie I have ever seen. I now feel like a new man and know that, win or lose, I should give the glory to God. I will go back to church, and when I have my kids I will do my best to teach them about God. I am praying every night and many times a day for God to show me the way. I have put my future in His hands. I no longer worry about when or what job I will land because I know God will do for me whatever His will is. I also pray many times a day for Him to heal the hate I have in my heart and let me forgive my ex-wife for what she has done. Please tell your church, thank each of them for that movie. And please pray for me.

(From a Christian leader in Albania)

Tonight we showed *Flywheel* for the first time in Albania with Albanian subtitles. It was wonderful! We've translated many films, but many said tonight that this was the best one yet! Many even had tears in their eyes at different parts. Integrity is a huge problem here in Albania. It was ruined by the efforts of communism, so this film was a help in bringing conviction in hearts that we Christians need to be serious about our family and work. Thank you very much for allowing us to translate this film.

(From the wife of a man who recently
dedicated his life to Christ)

My husband Bill grew up a Roman Catholic. He always professed that he was a Christian, yet I never believed that he had a real relationship with Jesus.

[When] your movie *Facing the Giants* came out in the theater . . . Bill and I went and he liked it. I really didn't know how it would affect him, but I was praying for his soul. Every day I prayed that he would have a close relationship with the Lord and that he would seek His counsel in his life and His guidance of our family. When *Facing the Giants* was released on DVD he bought it.

During all this he became aware of the first movie you had made, *Flywheel*. That was about two weeks ago and just before we got the movie one of his colleagues died suddenly. It bothered him when the preacher said he just wished he had known [the colleague]. Bill started thinking about who would officiate his funeral as there wasn't a priest or preacher that knew him either. Then we got the movie and we watched it and it was great!

We had not been to church for two years. On Saturday he decided that he and our oldest were going to church on Sunday. I would be working and our youngest was with my mother. He went to the Methodist Church down the road, and I called him that afternoon to see how it went. He said he really enjoyed it and that they had another service at 6 p.m. and he thought he might go back. He went back that night by himself and during the service he began to cry in church and he remembered the part in *Flywheel* and he gave his life over to God right there in the pew! That night he emailed the preacher and they saw each other that Monday and he told the preacher what happened and they prayed together.

He has gone out and bought a new Bible and has been reading every day since. I feel like I have a new husband! He reads the Bible in the morning before he gets out of bed, when he gets home from work, and before he goes to bed at night!

I wanted to send this letter to you because through your movies my husband realized how empty he was and he also said that your movies showed him he was missing something. He told me that night that he felt so guilty because he had spent all those years in church and . . . never in his life had he felt the Lord like he did that day in church. Thank you for your ministry and keep up the GREAT work because with GOD NOTHING IS IMPOSSIBLE!!

(From a parent at a Christian school in Colorado)

I had to tell you the news! My family watched this exceptional movie and it changed our lives. Then our school showed this movie to the staff and the next day they showed it to the junior and senior high kids and teachers. After it was over eight kids came to Christ. Teachers and students got up and asked for forgiveness from each other. They went to two periods and spent the rest of the day in a revival time all together, because of the message of this movie and the power of prayer.

We are now hosting a family fun movie night for the community and our preschool and elementary families. Free of course. Our school got all the appropriate forms from you all to do these things.

We have now formed a prayer team to pray for all of the students and staff, with eight volunteers. Our God is good!

Please make more movies! We're praying for that!

(From a youth pastor returning recently from Tajikistan)

Recently I returned from a country more than half way around the world, Dushanbe in Tajikistan. On my return, flying from Dushanbe, Tajikistan to Istanbul Turkey, on Turkish Airlines, your film *Facing the Giants* was shown. Keep in mind that the airline is owned and operated by Muslims, and everyone aboard the flight was of Arab decent. A fellow instructor and I were the only two non-Arabs on the plane.

It was absolutely inconceivable to show such a film to this audience and allow it to continue to the end, but it was shown to completion!

It was obvious to me [in Tajikistan] that God was in full

control. It seemed He was affirming this when this movie was shown on our return flight, indicating how He could do the incredible and impossible.

Thank you for the film!

Endnotes

Chapter 1: *Plowing the Field*
1.   Alan Redpath, *More Gathered Gold*, comp. John Blanchard (Hertfordshire, England: Evangelical Press, 1986), page 273.

Chapter 2: *Back-Door Revival*

1.   Vance Havner, *Pepper'N Salt* (Westwood, NJ: Fleming H. Revell, 1966), page 29.

Chapter 3: *Facing My Own Giant*

1.   Wayne Watson, "God in a Box," ASCAP Word Music/ Material Music, 1992.
2.   A. W. Pink, *Gathered Gold*, comp. John Blanchard (Hertfordshire, England: Evangelical Press, 1984), page 124.
3.   Warren Wiersbe, *Why Us? When Bad Things Happen to God's People* (Old Tappan, NJ: Fleming H. Revell, 1984), page 13.
4.   John Murray, *More Gathered Gold*, page 3.
5.   Charles Spurgeon, *The Westminster Collection of Christian Quotations*, comp. Martin H. Manser (Louisville, KY: Westminster John Knox Press, 2001), page 381.

Chapter 4: *An Environment of Prayer*

1. Andrew Bonar, *More Gathered Gold*, page 234.
2. A.W. Tozer, *More Gathered Gold*, page 95.
3. Ron Dunn, from a sermon he preached on "Mountain-Moving Faith" from Mark 10.
4. Charles Spurgeon, *More Gathered Gold*, page 99.

Chapter 5: *A Visionary Team*

1. Walt Disney quote and story are from Pat Williams with Jim Denney, *How to Be Like Walt: Capturing the Disney Magic Every Day of Your Life* (Deerfield Beach, FL: Health Communications, Inc., 2004), page 84.
2. Vance Havner, *Pepper 'N Salt*, pages 23–24.
3. John Mason, *Imitation is Limitation* (Grand Rapids, MI: Bethany House, 2004), pages 72–73.

Chapter 6: *Attitude Is Everything*

1. Tom Eliff heard this comment while on a trip to Russia in 2004.
2. Helen H. Lemmel, "Turn Your Eyes Upon Jesus," 1922.
3. Vance Havner, from a sermon he preached in 1971.
4. This quote has been widely attributed to D.L. Moody.

Chapter 7: *Relationships Are Essential*

1. Vance Havner, *Pepper 'N Salt*, page 82.

Chapter 8: *Plow the Field God Gives You*

1. This quote has been widely attributed to D.L. Moody and to Edward Everett Hale.
2. Tommy Yessick, *Sports Ministry for Churches* (Nashville: Convention Press, 1996), page 4.
3. Stuart Briscoe, quoted by Ron Dunn, *Victory* (Wheaton, IL: Tyndale House, 1984), page 11.

4. Ron Dunn, *Don't Just Sit There . . . Have Faith!*
    (Amersham-on-the-Hill, Bucks, UK: Alpha, 1994), page 212.

Chapter 9: *Growing Pains and Moviemaking*

1. Pat Williams and Jay Strack, with Jim Denney, *The Three Success Secrets of Shamgar* (Deerfield Beach, FL: Faith Communications, 2004), pages 66–67.

Chapter 10: *Connect with the Right People*

1. Joe Westbury, "MPAA 'PG' rating is a mixed blessing for Kendrick brothers," *Christian Index*, July 20, 2006).

Chapter 11: *Send the Rain*

1. Vance Havner, *The Secret of Christian Joy* (New York: Fleming H. Revell, 1938), page 67.
2. Vance Havner, *The Secret of Christian Joy*, page 68.
3. This quote has been widely attributed to Billy Sunday.
4. Vance Havner, *Sifted Silver*, comp. John Blanchard (Hertfordshire, England: Evangelical Press, 1995), page 264.
5. This quote has been widely attributed to C.S. Lewis.
6. Warren Wiersbe, *Be Alive* (Wheaton, IL: Victor Books, 1986), pages 91–92.

Chapter 12: *That's a Wrap*

1. Ron Dunn, *Don't Just Sit There . . . Have Faith!*

This book was produced by CLC Publications. We hope it has been life-changing and has given you a fresh experience of God through the work of the Holy Spirit. CLC Publications is an outreach of CLC Ministries International, a global literature mission with work in over 50 countries. If you would like to know more about us or are interested in opportunities to serve with a faith mission, we invite you to contact us at:

CLC Ministries International
PO Box 1449
Fort Washington, PA 19034

Phone: (215) 542-1242
E-mail: clcmail@clcusa.org
Website: www.clcusa.org

DO YOU LOVE GOOD CHRISTIAN BOOKS?
Do you have a heart for worldwide missions?

You can receive a FREE subscription to
CLC's newsletter on global literature missions
Order by e-mail at:

clcheartbeat@clcusa.org
or fill in the coupon below and mail to:

P.O. Box 1449
Fort Washington, PA 19034

FREE *HEARTBEAT* SUBSCRIPTION!

Name: _____

Address: _____

_____

Phone: _____ E-mail: _____

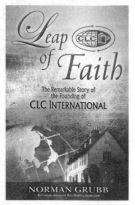

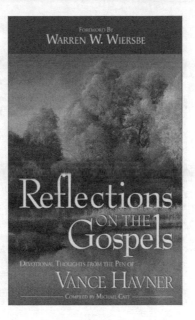

REFLECTIONS ON THE GOSPELS

Vance Havner

Compiled by Michael Catt

Rescued by Michael Catt from a collection of newspaper columns and compiled for the first time in book form, this wonderful devotional gives a unique insight into God's Word through the eyes of this great preacher.

Trade Paper ISBN 978-0-87508-783-2

FACING THE GIANTS

Novelization by Eric Wilson

Based on the original movie by Alex Kendrick & Stephen Kendrick

Available in book stores everywhere August 2007

Thomas Nelson, P.O. Box 141000, Nashville, Tennssee 37214

THE CALVARY ROAD
Roy Hession

Do you long for revival and power in your life?

Learn how Jesus can fill you with His Spirit through
brokenness, repentance and confession.

"This is one of the books that made the greatest impact on me as a
young Christian, and in the work of Operation Mobilization around
the world. We felt the message of this book was so important that it has
been required reading for all who unite with us.

"I would recommend every believer to read this book, and to follow
up on it by reading *We Would See Jesus*."

George Verwer, Operation Mobilization

Trade Paper ISBN 978-0-87508-788-7
Mass Market ISBN 978-0-87508-236-3

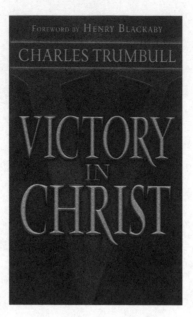

VICTORY IN CHRIST

Charles G. Trumbull

Trumbull reveals the full reality of the victory we have in Christ. Throughout the book Jesus is lifted up as the Victor over self and sin.

Trade Paper ISBN 978-0-87508-533-3

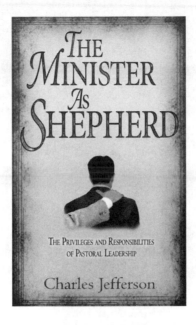

MINISTER AS SHEPHERD

Charles E. Jefferson

"You cannot be a good minister unless you have a shepherd's heart." Charles E. Jefferson takes an in-depth look at Scripture and history to uncover the shepherd's work, temptation and reward. This book will help you follow in the footsteps of the Great Shepherd.

Trade Paper ISBN 978-0-87508-774-0